Are Chief Executives
Overpaid?

The Future of Capitalism series

Deborah Hargreaves

Are Chief Executives Overpaid?

polity

First published in 2019 by Polity Press

Polity Press
65 Bridge Street
Cambridge CB2 1UR, UK

Polity Press
101 Station Landing
Suite 300
Medford, MA 02155, USA

ISBN-13: 978-1-5095-2779-3
ISBN-13: 978-1-5095-2780-9 (pb)

A catalogue record for this book is available from the British Library.

Library of Congress Cataloging-in-Publication Data

Names: Hargreaves, Deborah, author.
Title: Are chief executives overpaid? / Deborah Hargreaves.
Description: Cambridge, UK ; Medford, MA : Polity Press, 2018. | Includes
  bibliographical references and index.
Identifiers: LCCN 2018019580 (print) | LCCN 2018020871 (ebook) | ISBN
  9781509527830 (Epub) | ISBN 9781509527793 (hardback) | ISBN 9781509527809
  (pbk.)
Subjects: LCSH: Chief executive officers--Salaries, etc. |
  Executives--Salaries, etc.
Classification: LCC HD4965.2 (ebook) | LCC HD4965.2 .H47 2018 (print) | DDC
  331.2/81658--dc23
LC record available at https://lccn.loc.gov/2018019580

Typeset in 11 on 15 Sabon by
Servis Filmsetting Ltd, Stockport, Cheshire
Printed and bound in the United Kingdom by Clays Ltd, Elcograf S.p.A.

For further information on Polity, visit our website: politybooks.com

Contents

Foreword

One of my first assignments as a junior reporter at the *Financial Times* in Chicago in 1987 was to cover the Black Monday stock market crash. That October's steep decline remains the biggest single-day fall in US stocks. It was also an early lesson for me in the role of greed in our Western markets and capitalism.

The US investors in the late 1980s thought they had invented a form of insurance through the new derivatives markets that would insulate their port-folios from dramatic losses in the event of a stock market downturn. This gave them a false sense of confidence that risk was well managed. It led many brokerages and investing institutions to take more risks with their money in pursuit of high gains.

However, when the stock market fall came, it turned out that this so-called portfolio insurance not only did not protect their investments from losses, but actually exacerbated the decline. I was to witness this exuberance and neglect of the dangers in the build-up to many more market downfalls – right up to the banking crisis of 2008.

Greed has become one of the driving forces for many in our executive class, trumping long-term considerations about the future of their companies and the workforce, even overcoming fears about the fragility of capitalism itself. When there is the opportunity of enriching yourself to the extent that you and your family need never work again, who would not avail themselves of the option?

Policymakers, top public servants and academia have been sucked into the self-enrichment of the corporate elite and have sought to gain a piece of the action. Governments have been captured by business and failed to act on excessive pay at the top, politicians and public servants have sought careers in the private sector, and academics have bolstered the edifice while also feasting on the crumbs from the corporate table.

In this book, I am taking a look at how we built a super-elite class of multi-millionaire captains of industry and the implications this has for the economy, for the rest of the workforce and for us as a society. Soaring top pay and stagnating wages for the workforce have driven a sharp rise in inequality and fed perceptions of unfairness, undermining morale and faith in the system itself.

This analysis is a subjective description of what I have seen during my career and draws on lots of research done by the High Pay Commission which I chaired in 2010–11 and the High Pay Centre think tank which I set up in 2012.

Dysfunctional pay structures and the gulf between income for those at the top and the rest are not the inevitable products of late-stage capitalism. They are the outcome of choices made by governments and company boards about markets, incentives, tax rates and regulation. In many ways, they are also a fundamental misreading of human motivation.

1

Who Wants To Be a Millionaire?

In a world where just forty-two people have as much wealth as the poorest 3.7 billion and the lion's share of income generated in recent years has gone to those at the very top,[1] it is important to ask why the global economy operates in this way. Why have wages stagnated in developed countries, while stock payments, bonuses and dividends for those at the top have exploded?

Company bosses in most Western societies are cashing in untold riches for just a few years' labour in stark contrast to those who work for them, who have not had a real-terms pay rise for years.

The Brexit vote in Britain, the election of Donald Trump in the US, as well as the rise of populism in Europe, are commonly seen as an expression of frustration by those 'left behind' by the current economic structure and moves towards greater globalization. It is worth asking how late-stage capitalism in the West has created the conditions that hand so many benefits to the 'few': those at the top of the income scale and the wealthy.

The economic changes that have enriched the top 1 per cent have come since the 1980s and the rise in inequality over the past 25 years risks taking us back to a Dickensian-style divergence in incomes and lifestyles if we do nothing to reverse it.

One of the markers of growing inequality is the creation of the corporate multi-millionaire class – a relatively new demographic that was a rarity 20 years ago. It is the flood of income upwards into the hands of our business leaders that I want to explore in this book. This comes against the background of political choices favouring the corporate sector and policy decisions that have exacerbated a growing division between those running companies and those working for them.

In this chapter, we will explore the roots of the high pay culture, the justification that has been put up by a management elite intent on enriching itself and the way politicians have spurred them on.

Before the end of the first week in January, captains of industry in the world's leading economies will have notched up more income than the average annual wage. Their multi-million-dollar packages are so generous they only need show up for three or four days to pocket the same as the ordinary worker will take home over the year.[2] We're talking about the top elite here, those (usually men) running big multinational companies in the UK, US and across the developed world (with the notable exception of Japan). When people talk of inequality, they often refer to the top 1 per cent of incomes, but these chief executives are in the top 0.1 per cent.

Chief executives' pay has become part of a wider public debate about inequality across the developed world. But it is just as much about poor business practice, inefficient use of shareholders' funds and weak oversight. Put simply, many top bosses pay themselves millions just because they can. The high pay phenomenon has spread to other walks of life and top levels of pay in the private sector have had an impact in the upper echelons of the public sector. But this is mainly a private sector, big company issue.

This is also a very recent phenomenon. Executive pay has exploded in the past 20 years. Top bosses were always well rewarded, but the route towards independent wealth has only been open to them since the late 1990s. Thomas Piketty, the French economist who wrote the best-selling book *Capital* in 2015, calls them 'super-managers' who, for the first time in history, have the opportunity to become independently wealthy by spending a few years running a big company or a bank.

At the same time, a former head of the CBI business lobby in Britain has warned that managers have become so divorced from their own workforce that they risk being regarded as 'aliens' over pay. These 'aliens' have spawned a whole industry dedicated to justifying the rich rewards they incur.

As an elite, these executives are not homogeneous, but they generally share a belief in free-market economics, self-regulation and a small state. They are keen to see that governments share their preoccupations through generous funding donations (mostly in the US) and schmoozing policymakers.

The edifice built around managerial pay resembles more than anything else a religious cult with its own language, high priests and disciples. It even seeks to excommunicate critics who want to do more than say a prayer for reform.

How the numbers add up

Before we look at the reasons behind this surge in upper incomes, it is important to run the numbers to see how the most highly-paid men and women in

Britain and the US are grabbing an ever larger slice of the national cake.

In the UK and US, those in the top 0.1 per cent of the income scale currently pocket nearly 6 per cent of national income – a level last seen in the 1920s just before the Great Depression. In fact, we are living in the second 'Gilded Age', with billionaires increasing their wealth by a fifth in 2016 to a staggering $6 trillion. The Gilded Age refers to a period in the early 1900s when US families such as the Rockefellers and the Vanderbilts controlled vast fortunes.

I want to be quite clear when talking about the numbers though, that we are concerned in this book predominantly with incomes. Top pay is, of course, connected to wealth accumulation and is often used to mean the same thing, especially when entrepreneurs are paid little, but have large, lucrative holdings in their companies.

The distinction between wealth and income is blurred for very wealthy people as big incomes can quickly multiply when invested; money creates money. There are now 1,542 dollar billionaires in the world, many of whom will have built their fortunes through their business empires. Interestingly, these ultra-wealthy people are becoming concerned about the growing gap between rich and poor and whether there will be a backlash.

Are Chief Executives Overpaid?

This is a question at the heart of this book. It is important that the economy is seen to be fair or people will increasingly be drawn to the sirensong of populist politicians offering radical alternatives. It is therefore crucial that the business sector responds to moderate measures for reform or runs the risk of more dramatic consequences.

Upwards ever upwards

The trends in top pay are clear. The top 0.1 per cent of the most highly-paid people have made huge gains since the late 1990s, while elsewhere pay rises have barely kept up with inflation. Average chief executive remuneration increased in the UK from around £1 million in 1998 to over £5 million in 2015. It fell a little in 2016 to £4.5 million,[3] but it is too soon to say whether this is a reversal of the upwards trend, or a temporary blip. The ratio between average chief executive pay and employee pay was 129 to 1 in 2016, an increase from 48 to 1 in 1998. This means that a captain of industry in the UK takes home 129 times the annual income of someone on average wages.

In the US, the ratios are starker. In 2016, average chief executive pay was $13.1 million,[4] giving a pay ratio of 347 to 1. This compares to 42 to 1 in 1980. The most highly-paid executive in the US in 2017 was set to be Evan Spiegel, founder and chief executive of Snapchat, the technology firm, who pocketed $638 million even though the company has yet to make money. These figures are in the public domain, as companies listed on the stock exchange are required to publish pay figures for their executives in their annual reports.

In the UK, the totals account for realized pay, or what an executive actually receives in a particular year, even if it is an accumulation of performance-related awards that refer to past achievements, but are only paid out in that year.

There is another way of calculating bosses' pay that is generally in use in the US, and this is where some discrepancies arise. This other method is pay awarded in a particular year and is based on certain calculation models about how much that year's performance awards will be worth when they pay out. This means calculating the value of stock options and shares when they are eligible to be cashed in – in several years' time. Those running private equity companies, hedge funds and investment managers are not even subject to this level of scrutiny and rewards can be a lot higher, albeit below the radar.

The acceleration in pay-outs in the past two

decades is evident if you look further back to gain some perspective. At Anglo-US oil major, BP, its top boss was paid £143,334 in 1979 (just over £500,000 in today's money). By 2011, the package had risen to £4.45 million and then it made a huge leap to $19.6 million four years later (£14.9 million). After a revolt by shareholders, the company slashed the package by 40 per cent in 2016 to $11.6 million (£8.8 million). The ratio at the company between top pay and the average leapt from 16 to 1 in 1979 to 63 to 1 in 2011 and 148 to 1 in 2016.

These figures underline the shift in executive remuneration from a reasonably high middle-class salary thirty years ago to untold riches. If BP still paid its boss in line with previous levels, his pay would be much more modest. It would be similar to other professional positions in, for example, the army or medicine, as it was in the 1970s.

Changing climate ticks up top pay

The explosion in executive income is down to the convergence of many different factors that have changed the corporate sector over the years. These include globalization, expansion of companies across borders, the so-called international competition for top talent, the lack of a challenge to excessive awards, and of course, plain old greed.

If one dominant factor were to be cited, it would be performance-related pay and the incentives built around it. Performance pay has been a chief driving force in the acceleration of top rewards, against a backdrop of political choices that have served to exacerbate inequality since the beginning of the 1980s.

First of all, we need to take a brief look at the way companies are constituted and how these big pay packages are decided. Governments in recent times have tended to steer clear of too much regulation of big business, and most of the rules applying to the way companies are run are loosely bracketed under the term 'corporate governance'.

Corporate governance in the UK is non-binding, but applied on a 'comply or explain' basis, which means that you follow the guidelines and if you don't, you explain to your shareholders why not. In the US, the rules are more legalistic, but there are fewer of them and shareholders advise companies on governance standards.

A corporate scandal will often prompt a knee-jerk reaction by ministers – in the UK this takes the form of a corporate governance review by a member of the business elite, introducing a revised set of guidelines. This has happened many times since the initial UK corporate governance code was developed after a review by Sir Adrian Cadbury in 1992. In the US, there is generally a legal reaction such as the Sarbanes-Oxley Act, introduced after the Enron debacle.

How companies work

Most companies in the UK and US now follow conventional practice in setting pay rates for their top bosses. Executive rewards are decided by a handful of directors on the company's remuneration committee – a sub-group of the board of directors.

The board in many countries (with the notable exception of Germany) is made up of part non-executive directors and part executives who run the company. The non-execs are drawn from the ranks of the great and the good (many of them have several such jobs) and they are there to keep an eye on the management team, support and back them up where necessary, and also challenge them if need be.

The executive directors on the board in the UK are generally the chief executive, who runs the company, and the finance director; sometimes directors with other responsibilities such as human resources or marketing will sit on the main board. The British chairman for a big public company is a non-exec, although in the US he often runs the company as well.

From the ranks of these non-execs, the remuneration committee deliberates on pay. It will do this with the help of the company's human resources personnel and often will employ professional remuneration consultants to advise it. The remuneration committee meets two or three times a year. It sets pay with reference to performance targets, share price gains and other measures. In remuneration industry-speak, the chief executive's package is designed to 'attract, retain and reward', the top boss.

Remuneration committees are required to give consideration to pay and conditions in the rest of the workforce when setting executive levels. However, the amount of time devoted to this is small compared to the hours spent discussing the top executive awards.

Non-execs on the board, and particularly the remuneration committee, are also required to bear in mind that they are representing the owners or stewards of the company; the shareholders. Remuneration committee members should be consulting shareholders and their representatives regularly on executive pay.

Principal–agent problem

The need for a dialogue between directors and shareholders stems from academic work that was doing the rounds of US business schools in the 1970s. This work on the so-called principal–agent problem explored the relationship between so-called owners of a company – the principals (or shareholders) – and their agents (the management).

In the 1970s, shareholders had not done well out of the companies they invested in, and there was a feeling that managers were running them as their own personal fiefdoms. This was particularly the case in the US and UK, where independent shareholders were the dominant form of ownership. In continental Europe, family and institutional ownership of big corporations still held sway. Successive reforms were introduced to try and rein in the executives. So, for example, the independent non-executives were appointed with a view to keeping an eye on those running the firm.

Then an influential article by Chicago economists in the *Harvard Business Review* in the early 1990s stated that executive pay should be used to align chief executives' interests with what shareholders really cared about – i.e. share prices. This is when the idea of paying executives in company stock or in instruments that could be cashed in for shares began to be developed.

Money-making becomes sexy

This academic work was being done against the backdrop of the 'loadsamoney' culture of the 1980s, which heralded an era of self-gratification and the pursuit of material goods. This happened on both sides of the Atlantic with the economic boom ushered in by the Margaret Thatcher–Ronald Reagan reforms. Blatant money-making became culturally acceptable – even desirable – and the new mindset started to colonize the business world.

Mrs Thatcher and President Reagan swept aside many of the constraints on business and liberalized the economy in a celebration of corporate success. At the same time, tax rates were slashed. Ronald Reagan reduced the US top rate of tax from 70 per cent to 28 per cent and cut corporate tax from 48 per cent to 34 per cent. Similarly, when Margaret Thatcher became UK prime minister in 1979, she cut the top rate of income tax from 83 per cent to 60 per cent – seen at the time as a huge concession to top earners. During the course of her tenure, she cut corporation tax from 52 per cent to 35 per cent. Mrs Thatcher told a business conference in 1983 she wanted to create a 'Get-up-and-go, instead of a sit-back-and-wait-for-it Britain'. This meant creating a new culture she said; 'which accords a new status to the entrepreneur and offers him the rewards to match'.[5]

As they started to metamorphose from grey-suited apparatchiks to superstar bosses, the executives bought the rhetoric that they were worthy of heady rewards. The UK also became more Americanized as Mrs Thatcher feted the US entrepreneurial culture and sought to sweep aside the statism she perceived was holding back British business.

The cult of business saw leading figures like Jack Welch, chief executive and then chairman of General Electric, become celebrities, best-selling authors and management gurus. Jack Welch expanded GE from a market value of $12 billion to an enormous $505 billion on his retirement through a mix of acquisitions and sales growth. He was renowned for his often brutal style of management and for his huge share-based payments.

These men required a stake in the company,

it was argued by the consultants and theorists at the time. This would give them 'skin in the game', so that their own interests would be in line with those of the company and its ultimate owners, the shareholders. This translated into the trend towards performance-related pay that remains in place today. The argument is that if certain measures of company performance are met, bosses would be allocated shares or share options (which can be converted into shares) so that it would be in their interests to maximize the value of the company to the benefit of themselves and the shareholders. The side-effects of this policy were not recognized at the time and are still disputed today.

The move to pay managers in shares and to introduce performance criteria in the 1980s planted the seeds for the pay revolution that followed. This period also entrenched the version of capitalism in the US and Britain that focused on shareholder supremacy. In all subsequent reforms of corporate governance, policymakers on both sides of the Atlantic have seen fit to imbue investors with increasing powers and depend on them to monitor the activities of the corporate sector, even though they have sometimes been reluctant to wield their power.

Are Chief Executives Overpaid?

Recovering economy pushes up shares

In the 1980s, as leading economies sloughed off the recessions they were enduring, stock markets recovered and share prices rose: so too did the share-based packages of the businessmen who ran the companies on those markets.

This pay revolution was also a symptom of the move among some of the leading western economies – mainly the US and UK – to focus more of their resources on finance in Wall Street or the City of London. It was called the 'financialization' of the economy, or how everyone wanted to be paid like a banker.

With the opening up of the London Stock Exchange under so-called Big Bang reforms in 1986, large American investment banks moved across the Atlantic, bringing with them their culture of big bonuses. One veteran banker recalls how the US banks went on a frenzy of hiring and acquisitions and suddenly everyone became greedy. This culture leaked out of the City of London and into British boardrooms, where company bosses wanted their pay to be similarly performance-related.

It should be clear that there were political choices involved in unleashing a high-pay culture. Margaret Thatcher was elected in the UK amid a backlash against organized labour and was set on crushing trade union power to set free the supposed entrepreneurial spirits she wanted to foster among the corporate set. She also launched a series of privatizations of companies such as British Gas and British Telecom, which saw the former civil servants running these businesses suddenly pitched into the premier pay league.

Similarly, Ronald Reagan came to power during a period of deep recession and stagflation – characterized as double digit economic downturn accompanied by double digit rate of inflation – in 1981. He was convinced that tax cuts for the rich, deregulation of markets and business, and control of the money supply to counter inflation, would improve the economy for all through the so-called 'trickle-down effect'. President Reagan gave his name to the branch of monetarist economics he popularized – Reaganomics – but much of his legacy has since been called into question.

Time *men of the year*

The concentration of wealth among top businessmen has a long legacy in America but a look at the choices made by *Time* magazine for its person of the year illustrates a flood of value to the top in recent years. *Time* has featured five businessmen on its cover as person of the year since it began the practice in 1927 and all of them are representative of the era in which they were chosen. Walter Chrysler, who founded the eponymous car company, was profiled in 1928, and Harlow Curtice, president of General Motors, in 1955 – the year after GM became the first US company to post profits of more than $1 billion. After that was Ted Turner, who founded the TV channel CNN in 1991, Jeff Bezos, founder of Amazon, featured in 1999, and Mark Zuckerberg who started Facebook, in 2010.

Mr Chrysler was paid $1 million in 1920 and 1921 – a huge amount at the time – when weekly wages at the firm were $31. Mr Chrysler's annual income was 620 times that of his employees. By the 1950s, remuneration for top bosses had levelled off somewhat, with Mr Curtice earning $800,000 at his peak; with average pay at $3,301, he was taking home 242 times the norm. Ted Turner, who founded CNN, the first 24-hour cable channel in 1990, took home a salary of just over $1 million in 1995 with a bonus of $680,000. That year average wages were $24,705, so Mr Turner was taking home 68 times the norm. In 2013, *Fortune* magazine estimated his net worth at $2.2 billion.

These riches are dwarfed by the personal fortunes of today's technology entrepreneurs, however. In 2018, Jeff Bezos was the richest man in the world with net wealth of $115 billion, since he remains the largest shareholder in Amazon. Mark Zuckerberg takes a salary of only $1 from Facebook, but his shareholding in the social-networking company means he has a net worth of $73 billion. This is in the context of the stagnation in wages for the average American at just over $37,500 a year.

Business at the heart of government

One of the reasons for the huge growth in top pay in the West in the past 20 years is the establishment of the business culture at the heart of government. Business people have the ear of policymakers and are often able to skew decisions in their favour.

In his 2013 book *The Political Power of the Business Corporation*, Professor Stephen Wilks, shines a light on this development. Business people come and go between government departments and politicians join big companies. It makes it very hard for successive governments to challenge the high pay culture of big business. It also means the mantra of the market has reached into the heart of government around the world. Politicians have looked to business people to overcome the sclerotic workings of their own civil servants and departments. Top executives have been drafted in to run working groups, examine operational practices and even into government itself.

Donald Trump's former Secretary of State, Rex Tillerson, was the boss of oil major, ExxonMobil; his Treasury Secretary, Steven Mnuchin, is a former Goldman Sachs banker. In fact, Charles Schumer, the senate minority leader, says between them, Trump's cabinet had a net worth of $9.5 billion (before Rex Tillerson left).

In the UK, according to Professor Wilks,[6] 600 former ministers and top-level civil servants were appointed to over 1,000 different business roles between 2000 and 2014. This extends right up to the top of government, with former Labour Prime Minister Tony Blair earning up to £2 million a year as an advisor to US investment bank, JP Morgan. George Osborne, former Conservative chancellor is being paid £650,000 as an advisor to US fund management firm, BlackRock.

At the same time, hundreds of senior executives from business have been appointed to government departments. Government departments have also tended to be reorganized to more closely resemble a corporate structure. Goldman Sachs alumni regularly join the US government as Treasury Secretary. 'The proposition is not that corporations "lobby" or indirectly influence government, it is rather that they have "acquired" government, almost as a monopolistic corporation acquires a competitor', Professor Wilks says.

This makes the business and political elite almost one and the same. It means it is very difficult to get support for radical curbs on big business without facing strong opposition. This is what Labour's shadow chancellor, John McDonnell, may have been referring to when he told the Labour Party conference in 2017 that a 'radical' Labour government attempting to do things differently would face a range of challenges, and it was seeking to answer the question; 'about what happens when, or if, *they* come for us'. It appears, among other things, he was referring to a possible run on the pound by international investors.

As Labour looks to rein in the corporate world, it will soon discover how intertwined multinational businesses are. Globalization has meant that big business is increasingly mobile and can avoid a national clampdown by shifting jurisdictions.

As bosses' pay has exploded with very little brake, the nature of big business has changed a lot in the past 20 years. Multinational companies have tended to get bigger, expanding into new areas beyond their home country, taking over rivals and in the process, becoming more complicated. US business schools have driven the agenda towards remuneration firmly rooted in performance and this has spread around the world.

In order to run these increasingly global companies successfully, it has been argued that we need a new breed of top talent – one that is, of course, more expensive than in the past.

Rewarding top talent

The talk of top talent tends to be a smokescreen for increasing rewards. The argument goes that there is a small supply of people with the ability to run a big company. This increases their value and improves their position when negotiating contracts.

However, the argument is largely a self-serving one that is not borne out by reality. Those who maintain this view insist that business leaders are highly mobile and ready to quit their existing roles if offered more money by rivals overseas. Remuneration committees are worried that they will lose their chief executive to the competition

and therefore do not want to disappoint him (or sometimes her) on pay.

Since the US pays the highest rates to business leaders by a long way, the global talent pool argument suggests that those highly-competent managers who are unhappy with their pay in other countries would gravitate towards the US. However, this is seldom the case.

Upon further analysis,[7] there is little movement among the top ranks of management. International moves are made lower down the ladder, but top bosses tend to be older, with families who need to be accommodated. America tends to recruit few chief executives from outside its own ranks. Less than 1 per cent of top executives in the UK were poached overseas and 80 per cent were promoted from within their own company in 2013.

Data drawn from the Fortune Global 500 companies showed that out of 489 appointments, just four chief executives across the world were recruited by another company overseas while already working as chief executives. In North America, Japan, Latin America and Eastern Europe, not one chief executive was appointed from abroad. And yet, companies regularly use the argument that they are competing internationally for talented leadership material and therefore need to pay top dollar.

Are Chief Executives Overpaid?

Benefits for US executives can be astronomical, but few leaders from overseas make it into the top ranks of American business. While those running US companies can have an overseas background, they come to the US much earlier in their careers and progress upwards from there. While the US is at the top end of the pay scale for executives, the UK is second, then the rest of Europe behind us. In Japan, executives are often paid modestly compared to the West, but they generally have longer tenure and extremely good pensions.

The argument about the scarcity of top talent even falls down on its own economic terms. In any normal market of supply and demand, if the supply of something is scarce, the price rises temporarily, but there is usually a move to increase supply which brings the price back into equilibrium. It could be that there are plenty of people out there who could develop the skills to be a business leader, but they are not given the chance.

These top positions are usually filled by a coterie of head hunters from a list of the usual suspects. Head hunters argue that they need tried and tested people to run top companies, but they do not think more creatively about talent, and the jobs are rarely openly advertised.

Who sets top pay

It is also worth making an additional point about corporate talent since top pay is set by a remuneration committee of the board of directors at a company. The committee consists of several non-executive members of the board – often with expertise in the subject.

Members of remuneration committees for FTSE 100 companies are often drawn from similar backgrounds to the directors they are paying, and many are from finance.[8] This makes them comfortable with big figures and happy to justify top pay awards. It also reduces the chance of a challenge over excessive remuneration since there are few who speak out or even see a problem.

Remuneration committee members are well-paid too. Average pay for a remuneration committee member was £441,383 in 2015 (remember these are part-time jobs) – 16 times the average for the British employee. Of course, this is dwarfed by the millions on offer to the executives they are paying, but it is a sizeable amount and puts them in the same class, and often social circle, as the directors they are monitoring. Many of them are also very well connected within the corporate class itself. Research by the Trades Union Congress (TUC) found that of the 383 remuneration committee members for the FTSE 100, 246 (64 per cent) had at least one other position with another company. Of those, 33 were members of another FTSE 100 remuneration committee.

This interconnection can be seen in a positive light. It means that experience can be shared across the corporate sector, that understanding of pay practices and trends is widespread and that people have the knowledge and expertise required in a complex subject. However, it also fosters a kind of group-think, reducing the chances of a challenge to large awards since it could cause social embarrassment for those moving in the same circles as the executives they are rewarding. The TUC accuses remuneration committees of becoming out of touch with the rest of society and ratcheting up pay at the top of big companies.

As we have seen, the cult of top pay has created an enormous gap between executive earnings and everyone else. The case for paying top dollar has been bolstered by an elaborate web of justifications from the need to reward a small group of talented people to the alignment of managers with shareholders. Those at the top have created the terms of debate and generally brook little opposition. It is regarded as heresy to point out some of the flaws in the arguments for their stratospheric packages. Even the system of control has been captured by the executive elite, who are the ones running the corporate governance reviews when policymakers feel the need to bow to popular opposition to burgeoning rewards. In fact, governments have progressively emasculated the voices of opposition to the corporate elite, curbing trade union powers and allowing executive greed to run riot.

The driving force behind the explosion in top pay in the past 25 years is the trend towards performance-related awards. This has created perverse consequences for the corporate sector, society and even the executives themselves, as we will see in the next chapter.

2

Just Deserts?

It would have been fascinating to be a fly on the wall of the boardroom at UK housebuilder Persimmon when it became clear that the company's bonus scheme would pay out the enormous sum of £110 million to chief executive, Jeffrey Fairburn. It seems that the chairman, Nicholas Wrigley, argued for some of the riches to be donated to charity and then resigned in December 2017, stating that he should have done more to cap the bonus. The head of the company's remuneration committee also resigned.

Persimmon's share price had rocketed since the bonus scheme was established five years earlier, in large part down to the government's help-to-buy programme that subsidizes home purchases for young buyers. Critics of the bonus scheme – including some of the company's own shareholders – called it a government-subsidized pay-out. Housing charity Shelter said the bonus was enough to build a house for every homeless person in York where the company is based. Mr Fairburn, however, defended the share-based scheme, saying it had incentivized executives. After a couple of months of bubbling criticism, including from executives at rival house-builders, Mr Fairburn has said he will donate some of his bonus to charity and the company has reduced the pay-out to £75 million.

The problem here is that many executives who run large corporations are actually performing a bureaucratic rather than an entrepreneurial task, but they are being rewarded like those who build companies from scratch.

In this chapter, we will look at this issue of performance-related pay. Do these incentives really make executives work harder as Mr Fairburn has argued? Would they achieve the same rate of success without the offer of ever-increasing riches?

Wealth creators deserve rewards

In defending his £63 million bonus award in 2016, Sir Martin Sorrell, head of the international marketing firm WPP, said the company's market capitalization had increased by £10 billion over the past four years and the share price had more than doubled. 'Most of my wealth, if not all of it, is and has been for the last 31 years tied up in the success of WPP. So if WPP does well, I do well and others in the company do well. If we do badly, we suffer.'[1]

Sir Martin is unusual for a British chief executive in that he founded WPP and ran it for 32 years; this is much more usual in the US. Most UK chief executives are promoted up the ranks, but have never started their own venture. While Sir Martin is right to say that most of his awards are in the form of performance-related shares, he did also benefit from a salary and generous travel and accommodation expenses. These sorts of arguments for paying top dollar are not to be dismissed lightly. Sir Martin has made WPP a highly successful company employing many thousands of people worldwide.

Sir John Hood, who runs WPP's remuneration committee, also defends Sir Martin's pay as being totally aligned with shareholders' interests as it is mostly paid in shares. But Sir Martin regularly takes home 700–1,000 times the average for the rest of the workforce at WPP, and it is worth asking whether those employees also create value for shareholders. In a way similar to most big companies, the incentive schemes at WPP do trickle down the organization and 50,000 employees are awarded shares; however, these are a small fraction of the awards on offer at the top.

Shareholders have been grumbling about Sir Martin's remuneration for years. Over a fifth of them voted against his pay package in 2017. And WPP's shares proved not to be as buoyant as Sir Martin's pay. While Sir Martin received £48 million in 2016–17, the shares lost a quarter of their value on a global downturn in the advertising market. Sir Martin resigned in April 2018 after an inquiry into misuse of company funds.

What goes up, should come down

And here we come to a crucial critique of top pay. It is that remuneration goes up swiftly when share prices are increasing, but is not quick to come down when the share price deflates. This has led to accusations that remuneration committees adjust the goalposts to accommodate a change in the investment climate so that executives can receive their rewards anyway.

This was certainly the case at Carillion, the international construction giant that collapsed at the end of 2017 when it ran out of funds. In 2016 the remuneration committee relaxed the criteria under which executive bonuses could be reclaimed. This meant that bonuses could not be clawed back if the company went bust. A year later, it made its first warning that profits would not be as great as expected and collapsed six months after that.

There are also suspicions that during a period of difficulty for the economy, executives' performance targets are made less challenging. Certainly, in the past 20 years, executive pay has gone up much faster than the main stock market indices in which the big companies are quoted. And if performance-related pay was really doing what it claimed to do, i.e. increase company value, you would expect pay and shares to track each other fairly closely.

There is another major issue with performance-related pay in that executives are often judged on targets that extend over different periods, adding to the complexity of pay for top bosses over the years. Some shareholders suspect that complexity is used to obscure how much will be paid out, in order to avoid scrutiny. Some executives even admit that their own package is sometimes too difficult to fathom.

'I think even in the case of Rio Tinto, elements of our remuneration are so complex that even I struggle to understand it, and that is a big statement. It is an admission', Jan du Plessis, the chairman of mining group, Rio Tinto, told Westminster MPs at a select committee hearing on corporate govern-ance. It certainly is an admission from a leader of a big company that he struggles to understand its pay policy. It also begs the question as to why he has not done anything to de-mystify it.

But before we discuss the complexity further, it is important to untangle the different strands of pay that executives will be awarded as part of their overall package.

What constitutes an executive pay packet?

These typically include: a *base salary*, which for most bosses in the FTSE 100 is generally in the region of £800,000–£1 million with no link to per-formance or the share price. This is accompanied by a short-term incentive such as an *annual bonus* paid in either cash or shares.

Then comes a *medium-term incentive* such as deferred or matching shares, whereby the executive gets a share award for meeting certain targets or the company gives him an award of shares that match his own investment. *Long-term incentive plans* (or LTIPs) have been the big growth area in the past 10 years; these consist of shares, share options or both, running concurrently and usually awarded depending on performance against agreed targets over a three-year period. There is much discussion about whether the LTIPs should be tied to a longer performance period, and some investors now insist on five years. The Financial Reporting Council – Britain's corporate governance watchdog – is consulting on whether to change the guidelines to insist that these incentive plans should run over five years.

US executives are usually awarded grants of stock options rather than shares. These can be converted into stock at a certain point in the future. Options give the directors the benefits of a rise in the share price, but if shares fall, the options are worthless, and they do not need to convert them.

Many executives also benefit from a *self/co-investment plan*, whereby they buy shares in the company on the condition that the company will award them a matching number of shares. These arrangements are also subject to some performance criteria.

Lastly, executives will receive a payment into their *pension* plan or, increasingly, an annual amount of around £100–£150,000 in lieu of pension. Most executive pensions are at the limit of their tax-free contributions so many have just stopped paying into them.

Companies also often give other *perks* such as

health insurance, life insurance, gym membership, tax equalization, help towards housing costs, a car or driver and, in the case of fashion company Burberry, an 80 per cent discount on the clothing range. These benefits represent 2 per cent of the package – or £91,000 for the chief executive. For example, in 2016, housebuilder Taylor Wimpey's chief executive Pete Redfern received a 5 per cent discount on the price of a new home acquired from the company in Spain or the UK, which is limited to one new home a year. Cruise company Carnival's chief executive, Arnold Donald, had $100,000 worth of personal aircraft use.[2]

A larger part of the executive's package is now paid in shares rather than cash, and lately a bigger proportion of total pay – particularly bonuses and LTIPs – is subject to deferral periods. This means the executives are awarded their bonus or LTIP payment at the end of the one or three-year time frame, but have to wait a further period before they can trade the shares and receive any money. This deferral period to some extent protects the company, as if subsequent evidence of negligence or poor leadership emerges, the company can withhold payment. Some companies also impose clawback terms, so that bonuses can be reclaimed if mismanagement comes to light.

Are Chief Executives Overpaid?

Payment in shares

While the number of companies introducing bonuses and LTIPs has risen in the past 20 years, their value as a proportion of total pay packages has also increased. This has seen more executives striving to achieve performance-related pay targets, as these affect a higher proportion of their total pay. The value of cash bonuses for FTSE 100 top executives increased almost five times between 1996 and 2013, while the value of LTIPs rose almost nine times.[3] These increases did not result in a drop in the value of chief executives' salaries, however. The additional payments were simply added on top of base pay.

As the move towards performance-related pay has become well and truly entrenched in executive culture, it is important to ask what sort of value these captains of industry are being paid to create? We will see that – as in so much of the executive remuneration mantra – the issue of performance is fairly flexible. Also, many top bosses are judged on relatively short-term criteria such as share price rises, but some of the decisions they take to boost share prices over the short-term could have negative long-term consequences for the companies they are running and their workforces.

Just Deserts?

Performing relatively well

'CEO pay has massively outpaced anything with which it can even be remotely correlated, whether it be revenue, profits or share price. Not only that, but in many cases those at the top have garnered gargantuan rewards for gross failure', writes David Davis (Conservative MP for Haltemprice and Howden, who is now also the minister for exiting the EU) in an essay for the High Pay Centre.[4]

In order to judge their performance, most directors at top companies have their targets for annual bonuses linked to company profits and earnings per share (this is the company's net income divided by the number of outstanding shares). They are also linked to some individual 'personal' objectives.

For the bigger incentive plan awards, a majority of big companies link executives' pay-outs to total shareholder returns (TSR, or the total amount returned to shareholders; the capital gain in shares plus the dividends). This sounds sensible as it is based on gains for shareholders, until you look at the way companies often use this data. There has been a long-term practice of referring to relative TSR, which means the company's performance over a stated time period relative to another group of companies, or to an index such as the FTSE 100.

While this relative performance has been questioned by many critics, it still persists as a measurement today. So, for example, in a discussion of this issue at the select committee hearing between MPs and Jan du Plessis, chairman of Rio Tinto mining group, in 2017, Mr du Plessis was asked why the chief executive's pay went up by 25 per cent given that the company's revenues and shares were down. The answer was that compared to the rest of the mining sector, the company had done quite well even if it had not performed that well when judged against a wider share index.

Remuneration committees can often find a way like this to justify increases in executive pay. No other employees are likely to enjoy such a flexible measure of 'success'.

Rewards for failure

The issue of relative performance is an important one for critics of executive pay, and more egregious examples have been lambasted in the press as 'rewards for failure'. Relative performance is a roundabout way of thinking of success, so that rewards can be given even if a company is loss-making, as long as its losses are not as great as rivals.

Just Deserts?

There was, for example, the £1.2 million pay-out to former Tesco supermarket boss, Philip Clarke, after he left behind him a £263 million accounting scandal. There was also an outcry over a 20 per cent increase in pay for Bob Dudley, chief executive of oil company BP in 2016, after the company announced a huge loss. Shareholders voted against this, but it did not stop Mr Dudley receiving the money as the vote was not binding.

At US bank Wells Fargo, chief executive Timothy Sloan was awarded a 17 per cent pay increase in 2016 to $12.8 million in spite of an ongoing accounting scandal that has rocked the company. It was justified by pointing out that most of the award was paid in shares and it was the lowest among top US banks.

Time and time again, these kinds of claims are made for exorbitant rewards that have become far removed from reality.

Executives who rake in huge rewards year after year can also remain unchallenged in spite of signs of distress at the company they are leading. There is a sort of group-speak that takes over where it is unusual to break ranks and call out excessive awards.

It can often take a dramatic intervention from outsiders to shake up pay awards. For example,

Are Chief Executives Overpaid?

John Hammergren, chief executive of McKesson, the US drugs distributor, suffered a rare setback to his earnings in 2017 when shareholders, led by the Teamsters union, voted down his package at the company's annual meeting. Mr Hammergren, who has been in charge since 2001 and also chairman since 2002, has received some $692 million from the company in the past 10 years, including his share stake and bonuses. His package for 2017 was $20 million which was less than the $23 million in the previous year. But shareholders – including some of America's biggest pension funds – are concerned about the company's role in the current opioid crisis that is gripping the country, and its financial exposure over lapses in its distribution chain. The company agreed to a settlement of $150 million with several US states for not keeping a firm enough grip on its drugs distribution.

It is not clear whether Mr Hammergren will get his $20 million as the investor vote against it is only advisory. The company's compensation committee said it would conduct a full review of executive pay as a result of the vote. Shareholders were certainly angry: they also voted to strip Mr Hammergren of the chairman's role and replace him with an independent director.

Nevertheless, company boardrooms are risk-averse places and the riskiest issue for the remuneration committee is how to reward the chief executive so that he or she will not leave the company. If that person feels they are not valued or rewarded highly enough, they could walk out and the company will have an expensive recruitment process to find a successor, and they could even end up paying the new person more.

More money for posh macs

This is what has happened at the British fashion company, Burberry, over the past few years. When chief executive Angela Ahrendts – one of the few women to lead a top company – left to join Apple's retail arm in 2014, the chief designer, Christopher Bailey was promoted to become chief executive while remaining design chief.

The board was worried that Yorkshireman Mr Bailey would be poached by a rival and awarded him £10.5 million in shares that would pay out in 2017. Shareholders protested and just over half voted against his pay. Mr Bailey was, however, richly rewarded, and in 2017 received the £10 million shares and £3.5 million in additional remuneration as well as his 80 per cent clothing discount. This time a third of investors voted against the package. In response, the company appointed a new chief executive, Marco Gobbetti, and Mr Bailey was given the title of president while remaining chief designer. Pay and bonuses were reduced to reflect a downturn in the company's core markets. However, in late 2017, Mr Bailey announced he was leaving to pursue other ventures.

This raises the question as to whether remuneration committees can buy loyalty to a company with a big share package, if as soon as that package vests, the executive is off to pastures new. If Mr Bailey had not received the share promise, would he have left sooner?

Also, if payment in shares is meant to give executives 'skin in the game' and make them think like shareholders, this is not always a defence against corporate meltdown. Dick Fuld, former chief executive at Lehman Brothers, the bank that collapsed in 2008 and almost took the entire US economy with it, received most of his $484 million package in shares. In Congressional hearings on the financial crisis, Mr Fuld defended his supposed rewards over eight years by saying that 85 per cent of it was in Lehman Bros' shares which he didn't sell, and subsequently became worthless.

It can be argued that there is little a chief executive can do to influence the global attitude to a company, so that when WPP encounters an advertising slowdown and Burberry sees Asian customers turn to something new, the executive team has little room for manoeuvre. But this argument can cut both ways; if executives have little control over the share price on the way down, how can they also control it on the way up? Is it therefore appropriate for them to reap the rewards of a rising share price in a buoyant business climate?

How much effect do chief executives have?

In interviews for the High Pay Centre about executive performance, many interviewees who were company directors, academics and commentators pointed out that executives were seeing their individual finances and reputation boosted just because they happen to have presided over a successful company that may have achieved equivalent success without their presence at the helm.

'The role of the CEO is often overstated', says long-term business leader Sir Philip Hampton, current chairman of pharma group GSK, who was at the time chairman of bailed-out bank RBS. 'Many CEOs are in charge of operations which would run quite smoothly without their daily input.'[5] Sir Philip was referring to the infrastructure that is in place around a chief executive and how this bolsters and supports his role, as well as the myriad of other directors and managers with similar skills who also help to create a successful company.

Whole academic treatises have been written on the importance of a leader of a business organization and whether they can make or break the company. There are examples of spectacularly bad chief executives who have damaged a company and others who have transformed it into a successful enterprise.

However, Swiss academic Professor Phil Rosenzweig, says: 'Minds leap very quickly from outcomes to causal attributions. We are quick to say that a successful company has a brilliant, charismatic CEO because we attribute success to the most visible person. The reality is much more complex.'[6]

Nevertheless, executives are accountable for what happens at a company. If they are lucky enough to preside over a period where things are going well, they reap the rewards. But equally, the buck stops with them when things go wrong and they are ousted. That doesn't always stop them being paid, however: the chief executive of Carillion was due to be paid nearly £700,000 for a year after stepping down from the outsourcing group in 2017, although this was cancelled when it went bust.

Luck is important

'Sometimes you just get lucky', Sir Philip Hampton told the High Pay Centre. 'Perhaps you joined an industry at the right time, maybe you were promoted at the right time, and then the circumstances of your industry suddenly become favourable. Even if you are a half-wit, you are going to do quite well in this situation. So many financial incentives rely on luck, the evolution of markets, rather than people's contribution.'[7]

This differs depending on the sort of market you are operating in. For example, a sustained period of demand for imported minerals from China is going to boost the fortunes of mining companies around the world with little input from their executives.

However, Sir Philip does not believe that performance-related pay should be altered to take account of luck and circumstance. 'You can never eliminate the element of mere participation in success and failure', he says. 'You should try and mute that element as much as you can. But sometimes in life, you have to say: "sometimes you are lucky and sometimes you are not"'.

Lord Wolfson, who is the chief executive of retailer Next, believes that luck only lasts so long, however. 'In the short term, a large business will run itself, but in the long run a company's destiny relies on the person at the top. If you let things happen automatically, you will eventually fail because no formula lasts.'[8]

This brings us to the issue of long-term performance. One of the criticisms of current pay structures is that so-called long-term incentives are anything but. Many LTIPs stretch over a three-year period, which is not considered long enough by many critics. Investors have increasingly started to stipulate a five-year appraisal process for a long-term performance plan.

Tim Martin, who founded the pub chain JD Wetherspoon, told the High Pay Centre that short-term measurement criteria may not only be deceptive, but can also be harmful to the company, with self-interested executives pursuing counter-productive strategies for personal gain. He believes that: 'a five-year perspective will lead CEOs to reduce costs, for example, in order to increase both earnings per share over that period and the resulting executive remuneration, even though this may have an adverse effect on the company itself.' Share prices can be manipulated in the short term to achieve spectacular returns for top bosses, but in the long term, the share price should reflect the quality of the leadership. Mr Martin said: 'The entire structure of corporate pay is based on performance over one, three or five years, when 10, 15 or 20 is more important.'[9] The problem for many chief executives is that their tenure does not last that long. The average term for a British chief executive is five years, so if they want to make their mark, along with their fortune, they need to get a move on.

In the US, they can last a lot longer if they are keeping the share price buoyant. Since US executives are often paid with large options packages, they do not bear the brunt of taking big risks to increase the share price (if shares fall, their options will just be worthless), but they can reap spectacular gains for boosting stocks.

Remuneration consultants

When remuneration committees are deliberating about executive pay, they are assisted by another key constituency: remuneration consultants. If executive pay is akin to a religious cult, the pay consultants are the high priests, writing the commandments on pay and signing up true believers. As legendary US investor and one of the richest men in the world, Warren Buffett, wrote to his shareholders in 2007: 'CEO perks at one company are quickly copied elsewhere. "All the other kids have one" may seem a thought too juvenile to use as a rationale in the boardroom. But consultants employ precisely this argument, phrased more elegantly of course, when they make recommendations to comp [compensation] committees.'[10]

Consultants are hired by remuneration committees to inform them about the latest trends in pay-setting, provide specialist advice on the design of a pay package and to ensure that pay is more closely aligned to shareholder returns. Individual directors may want to hire a consultant to provide them with information on their package and whether it is appropriate.

Consultants are often blamed, however, for pushing pay ever higher by a process known as benchmarking: where the consultants provide a table of similar executives to compare pay with. There is a suspicion that executives earning more than the person being benchmarked are cherry-picked for comparison purposes, adding to the ratchet on top pay.

Critics also claim that consultants can add complexity to the pay package, making it more difficult to understand. The consultants defend themselves by saying that they are there to ensure performance conditions are exacting and in line with the company's strategy. They claim that complex performance goals are important in aligning an executive's work with the aims of shareholders.

One thing for sure is that there is an army of advisers all looking to provide services to the board. Remuneration consultants are often part of big accounting firms, also providing other functions such as auditing services or pensions advice. The fees for this advice are not always disclosed. It is also not clear whether there is a conflict of interest between advisers offering lucrative auditing work who could shy away from suggesting that executive pay be reduced for fear of losing a profitable customer for their other services.

In evidence submitted to the select committee inquiry into corporate governance, institutional investment group Standard Life said: 'The use of advisers has become too commonplace and the incentives of many of these advisers are not aligned with good outcomes for companies, shareholders, employees or broader society.'

While the consultants defend themselves from the

charge that they are responsible for pay escalation, they can certainly be held accountable for spreading trends in remuneration practices. They also have a vested interest in the complexity of executive pay since a broad-brush simplification – as is recommended by many – would reduce the importance of their role.

The ratchet effect

Consultants have been blamed for another development that has helped push top pay ever higher: the so-called ratchet effect. This is part of the benchmarking process. Consultants produce data for remuneration committees showing how their chief executive fares compared with his peers and competitors at other companies. This is supposedly to place the executive among the ranks of others to ensure he does not miss out on the riches on offer. Of course, this is not the way it is described, but it is interesting that the advice tends to be one way – few consultants suggest a reduction in chief executive pay.

The ratchet effect comes from the tendency of the consultants to divide the executives into a ranking. They can then pinpoint the top quartile, or the top 25 per cent of most highly-paid executives in a peer group. Most remuneration committees want to signal to their chief executive that he or she is highly valued. They therefore want to pitch their offer into the top quartile of pay packages. Some of them feel that anything below this level is tantamount to indicating the chief executive is not good enough.

However, if all companies engage in this process, executive rewards will continue to spiral upwards with little check. A highly public example of where this went spectacularly wrong for a company came in 2014 when a British-based oil and gas explorer, BG Group, was looking to hire a new chief executive. The company was spun out of British Gas, the public utility in the UK when it was privatized, and it subsequently expanded internationally.

In 2014, it approached Helge Lund, a Norwegian who was running the state resources company, Statoil. It offered him a package that was worth £29 million to make the move – many times greater than his pay at Statoil even though BG Group was much smaller. The package included over £10 million in shares and a £480,000 relocation package. Even by executive pay standards, this package was seen as excessive. Shareholders were not happy and many voted against it. The Institute of Directors called the package 'excessive and inflammatory'. However, BG

Group stuck by its offer with a few tweaks. Chair of the remuneration committee Sir John Hood (who is also chair of WPP's remuneration committee) would have looked at other worldwide explorers when judging what to offer. He would have been aware that Rex Tillerson, who ran ExxonMobil, was paid around $25 million.

In the end, BG group, which had lost the support of some of its major shareholders, was taken over by Shell and Mr Lund ran the company for less than a year, but picked up some £15 million for doing so. Mr Lund's package at BG Group was some ten times larger than he was earning in his native Norway, where state-owned Statoil does not seek to compete in the global high-pay stakes even though it is extremely successful and five times bigger than BG.

Superstar executives

Sometimes companies get fixated on the idea that they require a 'Superstar' CEO to run their company and that no other person will do. This cult of the superstar is a fairly recent phenomenon and follows the greater press focus on businesspeople that developed in the 1980s.

However, as we have seen, the role of just one person can often be overstated. Companies would often do just as well to recruit from within their own ranks, where promotion is much cheaper than buying in a superstar from outside. It is also not necessarily the case that a prominent businessperson who has achieved significant success at one company will be able to replicate it at another.

Sceptics point to the example of Marc Bolland, a veteran executive who turned around Wm Morrison supermarket group when it was going through a difficult period. He was hired in 2009 to work the same magic at Marks & Spencer on a £15 million package. The press dubbed him the billion-dollar man, representing the fall in the value of Morrisons' shares and the rise in M&S after the announcement. But he failed to work the same effect on M&S, and by the time he announced his retirement six years later, profits were lower than when he started, in spite of a huge programme of capital spending.

Chief executives are only human; they cannot be expected to work wonders against the trend in the economy. Sometimes they are lucky and preside over huge share price gains which also benefit their own pocket, but they expect to reap the rewards even when times are tough. Their performance is defended by an elaborate system of justifications that have been developed around the top pay racket. Employees at other levels do not benefit from this sort of discretion and struggle to see why the top boss is paid millions for just turning up to work.

The growing move towards share-based payments has also given top executives perverse incentives, of which we will see more in the next chapter.

3

Why Top Pay Matters

Most bosses would need several lifetimes to spend their earnings. There are only so many superyachts and ski chalets to acquire. And we could ask why not? Haven't they earned it by creating value in their companies and doesn't that wealth trickle down through society, lifting others with it? Politicians have always been fairly relaxed about tackling soaring executive pay when the economy was doing well and incomes across the board were up.

There is a ratchet effect here too. The modern economy has succeeded in turning peoples' needs (the basic material goods required to achieve a secure standard of living) into wants which are never-ending. This has created an insatiability for ever-more rewards. 'Material wants know no natural bounds, they will expand without end unless we consciously restrain them', say Robert and Edward Skidelsky in their book: *How Much Is Enough?*[1]

In this chapter, we will explore why performance-related pay has not achieved what it set out to do, and how executives have been rewarded many times more than the value they have created. We will also look at why paying people like this can have perverse consequences for them, the wider corporate sector and society as a whole.

Performance-related pay is anything but

If performance-related pay really worked, you would expect to see an enormous rise in the success of British and US companies over the past 20 years as pay over that period has soared. Given the claims for performance pay, you would expect to see the chief executive's rewards rising in tandem with the share price, profits and shareholder returns.

In reality, executive pay has far outstripped any of the measures of company performance with which it is meant to be correlated. Performance-related pay is often poorly designed, does not always align with the long-term interests of the company and can create perverse incentives. Any effect it has is weak and it is very difficult to isolate the contribution of an individual to the success or otherwise of the company as a whole. Recent research shows either no relationship or, at best, a weak link between directors' pay and company performance.[2] It is very difficult to find a correlation between company pre-tax profits or earnings per share and bonus payments even though these are important criteria for judging the annual pay-outs. Similarly, there is little correlation between LTIP share awards and the changes in total shareholder return or earnings per share over the three-year length of the plans.

In a longer-term analysis running from 2000 to 2013, increases in nearly all of the key elements of FTSE 350 directors' remuneration far outstripped the corporate performance measures they were generally tied to. So, for example, directors' pay rose by nearly 350 per cent during that period compared with a 140 per cent increase for revenues and 195 per cent uplift for pre-tax profits. It seems that on the basis of this data, shareholders are, at the very least, overpaying chief executives to achieve the sort of outcomes they want.

David Davis MP points to the growing chasm between achievement and reward as being particularly evident in the banking sector. Research on the US financial services industry indicates that despite its fast computers and credit derivatives, the current financial system is no better at transferring funds from savers to borrowers than the financial system at the start of the twentieth century. 'And yet the compensation of "financial intermediaries" as a fraction of GDP is at an all-time high – around 9% of GDP.'[3]

However, it should be said that there is still contentious debate about this issue, as there are other ways of measuring the link between pay and performance. It is not an exact science since establishing a connection between the two can vary depending on the period over which you measure and where you set the baseline.

The whole debate about whether executives are really creating company value and returns for shareholders is likely to rage on for some time to come. And, let's face it, the argument over whether performance-related pay works is unlikely to be won on the numbers alone. It is a highly emotive issue and bound up with the executives' sense of self-worth.

There will always be other statistics to quote that show it is working well. Indeed, this is what remuneration consultants spend a lot of their time doing. But we could say it is the wrong debate to be having. If we are trying to pay senior management for such a complex job as running a big, multinational company, are we not trying to reduce their input to certain crude measures that fail to capture what they really do on a daily basis? Are we actually asking our corporate leaders to do the right thing by trying to link their pay so closely to their company's fortunes? Is a focus on profits and share price really the one we want at the forefront of our captains of industry's minds?

Short-term consequences of performance pay

There are consequences to how we pay chief executives beyond whether they are giving value for money. By encouraging them to focus on the share price in particular, we are giving them a very short-term obsession with just one measure of company success.

A short-term approach by business is a long-time obsession of governments in the UK and US, and they are always looking at how to lengthen the attention span of the corporate sector. In a review on short-termism for the UK coalition government in 2012,[4] Professor John Kay characterized short-termism as a tendency to underinvest whether in physical assets or in product development, employee skills and reputation with customers. He also described hyperactive behaviour by executives with a corporate strategy focused on restructuring, financial re-engineering or mergers and acquisitions at the expense of developing the business. In this way, he details the long-term damage that can be wrought on the company by putting too much of a short-term focus on the shares.

If your package is dependent on reaching a certain share price, but there is little you can do to affect that share price, you could see that you would be tempted to use the tools within your reach such as suppressing the wages bill and other costs, in order to boost shares. Executive remuneration has exploded in recent years while workforce wages have stagnated – could this be the reason?

In fact, there is another, equally pernicious outcome of a short-term focus on shares. Academic studies have pointed to the tendency for executives to manipulate earnings or otherwise disguise the true profit figures, if their pay is dependent on stock prices over the short term.

Share buybacks

A large number of US and UK companies have engaged in a form of manipulation of their share prices in recent years by buying back their own shares on the open market. Executives often use a dip in the stock market to venture in and buy back a tranche of their company's shares. These are then cancelled, leaving the pool of available shares on the open market smaller and therefore, higher in price. This benefits the executive directly when he or she is paid mainly in shares or options.

Share buybacks have received a lot of attention on both sides of the Atlantic in recent years, with the *Economist* magazine dubbing them 'corporate cocaine'. US companies have spent a staggering $2.2 trillion on buybacks since the turn of the century. The justification for them is that it makes sense to convert expensive equity into cheap debt when interest rates are low. But they have come at vast cost, incurring large borrowings or diverting funds that could be spent on investment in new plant and machinery, new technology or even in training and increasing the skillset of the workforce.

Buybacks have also been criticized by management experts as the refuge of a chief executive who has run out of ideas. The opprobrium around them prompted the British government to announce an inquiry into buybacks in January 2018 over concerns they were being used 'to artificially inflate executive pay'.

While the uplift in the share price from buybacks usually lasts long enough to boost the directors' share-based bonuses, it tends not to be that long-lasting, so is generally not a good use of company funds from a long-term shareholder's point of view.

What chief executives really want

While executives will often manoeuvre to increase their pay-outs, it can be argued that we are giving them the wrong incentives. At its heart, the culture of executive remuneration fundamentally mistakes the motivation of the individual. Money, after all, is not everything. In fact, it could be argued that using only money to motivate people is a dereliction of duty and evidence of poor management. This was the conclusion of a review by lawyer Anthony Salz into wrongdoing at Barclays bank in 2013. Mr Salz said Barclays was too focused on profits and bonuses rather than the interests of customers. Instead of managing bankers, Mr Salz suggested that senior management had depended too much on the bonus culture to reward them, creating an overwhelming focus on money.[5]

Excessive risk-taking by bankers in pursuit of higher bonuses was also implicated in the failings of the banking system in 2008, which caused the financial crisis – the consequences of which we are still dealing with today.

But not all bankers and top bosses are bonus-obsessed. John Cryan, shortly after his appointment as chief executive at Germany's Deutsche Bank, told a conference in Frankfurt in 2015: 'I've no idea why I was offered a contract with a bonus in it because I promise you I will not work any harder or any less hard in any year, on any day because someone is going to pay me more or less.'[6] 'I've never been able to understand why additional excess riches drive people to behave differently', he said. Mr Cryan is asking a perennial question posed by ordinary people when they look at the rewards on offer to senior executives. Quite rightly, ordinary employees might ask why the boss needs a million-dollar bonus to do a good job when they are required to complete their roles effectively for a fixed salary – and, indeed, one that has barely risen in recent decades.

Mr Cryan may be unusual in not being driven by money. His comments were decried by some other bankers when he made them and certainly greed and the drive for higher bonuses continue to motivate many. But Mr Cryan is not alone. At the High Pay Centre, we did a survey of members of the Institute of Directors, and asked them: 'What is the most important driving force for executives?' Only 13 per cent answered financial reward. By far the largest number – 54 per cent – said building a successful company was the most important factor.[7] Executives are obviously driven to some extent by the personal rewards on offer, but beyond that, many want the satisfaction of creating value for a broader community.

Indeed, Helena Morrissey at Legal and General Investment Management, said the same to the MPs on the select committee: 'It [high pay] is a driver, and clearly for key executives they will want to work somewhere where they are well remunerated for their contribution. ... However, most people who are executives would honestly say that they do it for more than just the money. There is a sense of satisfaction that they are creating value for a broader community.'

It's not all about money

This fits in with other research on executive pay, suggesting that highly-skilled people in positions of key responsibility, already well-paid in comparison to wider society, are not motivated by the prospect of even more money. While greed is a factor in securing riches, many executives also look beyond the issue of more wealth.

The work of chief executives is unsuited to performance-related pay according to a recent article in the *Harvard Business Review*. It says that this sort of motivation is intrinsic: business leaders are doing it for satisfaction and a sense of achievement. On the other hand, when people are extrinsically motivated, they do things because they will receive greater rewards. 'And when financial incentives are applied to increase senior leaders' extrinsic motivation, intrinsic motivation diminishes.'[8]

Professor Alexander Pepper, who has looked into the behaviour of top executives and the way they are motivated, agrees. He says 'intrinsic [i.e. non-pecuniary] motivation is a significant factor that drives executives.'[9] Professor Pepper, along with his former employers at PwC, has surveyed executives around the world and found that they would be prepared to give up on average nearly 30 per cent of their income to work in more intrinsically satisfying jobs.

What really appears to motivate company executives is status. This is important for all of us – even students who are not yet in the world of work respond in similar ways to top bosses about the 'perceived fairness of reward'. Most executives would prefer to receive a lower absolute amount of pay, provided that it compares favourably with their peer group, rather than a higher amount that leaves them badly-off compared to the peer group, according to research conducted by Professor Pepper. There are differences between executives in different countries, but these behavioural characteristics are largely universal and not affected by cultural factors.

Status seems to be a fundamental human motivation which, in fact, has little to do with money. It suggests that other, non-pecuniary ways of rewarding the well-paid could be equally effective in motivating them. There are some companies that have tried giving high-ranking employees rewards in the form of ringside seats to top sporting or theatrical events.

Other research by Professor Pepper also undermines the argument that top executives need ever bigger carrots dangled in front of them to improve their work ethic. He has found that executives 'are much more risk averse than standard economic theory would suggest'. This means they value a 'sure' thing such as money more highly than a risky option such as the promise of a share award.

At the same time, 'executives are very high time

discounters'. This means that if they know they will not get their share award for another three years, they disregard its value. 'This empirical evidence challenges conventional wisdom about the merits of high-powered incentive plans and pay for individual performance. It suggests that long-term incentives may actually be fuelling increases in executive pay, rather than helping to contain pay inflation.'

In other words, boards have made their performance offers to executives stretch over the longer term (generally three years) in order to balance remuneration and ensure bosses are suitably motivated, but because the executives discount these awards, they have had to make them higher and this has helped fuel the pay explosion.

At the same time, if executives are fixated on status, it would suggest that however much they are paid, it will never be enough unless others are paid less. But it might also mean that other ways of rewarding them, that mark them out as special in some way, can be just as effective. This might require a move away from targets, since an obsession with performance can weaken it, and it is better for individuals to focus on learning, rather than performance or outcome goals.

Nevertheless, performance pay is deeply entrenched. Reuters, the information group (now

Thomson Reuters) was the first company in Britain to introduce LTIPs in 1993 and by 1995, this had spread to most big companies. In the next 20 years, executive remuneration really took off.

How top pay keeps down productivity

There is a strong argument to be made that the structure of top pay awards is damaging to the economy. Andrew Smithers, the respected City economist, has argued cogently that executives' focus on share-based returns is a reason for the poor productivity record of the UK economy. His 2013 book *The Road to Recovery* puts his argument forward.

Executives have been given short-term incentives to cut costs and hold down investment in innovation so that profits and share prices go up. This has caused serious detriment to the UK economy, Mr Smithers argues. UK productivity has not increased since the financial crisis and in 2016, British workers produced 15 per cent less per hour than workers in other G7 countries.

Of course, one way for executives to keep costs under control is to suppress the wage bill for the workforce. At a time when employment is buoyant, economists have been puzzled by the lack of inflation in average wages which are lower now in real terms than they were ten years ago. Wages in the UK and US remain below the levels of before the financial crisis in 2007–8. In the US, median household income is $59,039 – still below the point it reached in 2000, of $60,399.

Mr Smithers says there is a high probability that the decline in corporate investment that has been witnessed in recent years is a result of the change in the way management has been paid. Investment in fixed assets in the UK has fallen from 11 per cent of GDP in 1997 to 7 per cent and continues to decline. The dramatic fall in labour productivity has probably been caused by the management focus on short-term cost-cutting. This means that the prospect for growth over the medium term is very poor unless business revives its investment strategy.

So, under Mr Smithers' analysis, performance-related pay for senior managers and its focus on share price improvements is causing direct damage to the UK economy.

The TUC has argued in a similar vein that the suppression of wages by top management has been equally damaging to a workforce that is seeing its living standards squeezed. In 2017, the TUC reported[10] that Britain ranked 103rd out of 112 countries for pay growth since the financial crisis. Based on data from the International Labour Organisation, Britain was ranked 103rd with a fall in real wages of 1 per cent, and the US 76th with a small rise of 0.5 per cent.

Interestingly, Scandinavian countries, where inequality has traditionally been lower and executive pay is not in the top league, were the highest ranked countries for wage growth in western Europe, with Sweden at 52nd place with a 1.8 per cent wage growth and Norway at 56th with 1.6 per cent.

TUC General Secretary Frances O'Grady said: 'UK workers suffered one of the worst pay squeezes in the world after the financial crash. And with food prices and household bills shooting up again, another living standards crisis is a real danger.'[11] It can be argued that by channelling the bulk of awards to the top and suppressing wages for everyone else, we are holding back the economy. Top bosses tend to save their money or invest it in financial assets such as stocks and shares, whereas if it were spread more evenly throughout the population, we would add back spending power to the economy.

The UK and US economies are currently afloat on a sea of debt as ordinary people borrow on attractive credit terms to maintain their lifestyles against a squeeze in their take-home pay. This is clearly not sustainable over the long term. Interest rates have been at historical lows for ten years, which is unprecedented in history, and at some point, the public will have to be weaned off cheap credit.

When the workforce sees its rewards stagnate while those at the top carry on enriching themselves, there is a big gap in credibility that opens up between our business leaders and the rest of us. This has important implications for the policy debate in Western economies and, indeed, can undermine faith in free markets and our current form of capitalism.

Pay disparities damage morale and business reputation

Big pay gaps lead to disenchantment at work and poor outcomes for the workplace, as evidenced in a report by the Chartered Institute for Personnel Development. In a survey published in December 2015 the CIPD found that 6 out of 10 employees were discouraged by the high levels of chief executives' pay and felt it was bad for a company's reputation.[12]

Nearly half of employees (44 per cent) felt their boss's pay was either far too high or too high and a majority favoured more pay transparency at their company. 'These results show that UK employees believe the negative impact and consequences of current CEO pay levels are far-reaching.' Indeed, speaking to an employee at a bank branch about bankers' bonuses, he told me it was outrageous how much the top boss was paid when many in the branch were struggling to make ends meet. 'I just undermine them in any way I can', he admitted.

Even business people themselves are concerned that public unease over executive pay levels has damaged the reputation of the corporate sector and undermined their license to operate. In a poll of the Institute of Directors (IOD) in 2015,[13] 52 per cent of those answering (out of 1,089) believed that anger over levels of senior executive pay posed the biggest threat to public trust in business. This topped the poll as the perceived biggest threat to public trust in the sector.

The then director-general of the IOD Simon Walker said that he believed performance-related pay can be 'a key driver of success'. 'However, in some corners of corporate Britain pay for top executives has become so divided from performance that it cannot be justified. Runaway pay packages, golden hellos, and inflammatory bonuses are running the reputation of business into the ground. Large companies need to look closely at the role excessive pay is playing in fuelling an anti-business backlash from the public and some politicians'.

Mr Walker's words were prescient as the corporate sector is now so distrusted and discredited over pay and other scandals that people tend not to believe businesspeople when they talk about important policy issues. So, for example, when business warned about the dangers of Brexit, they were ignored. And tellingly, when government called on retailers to warn about rising prices as a result of Scottish independence during the referendum in 2015, they were actively ridiculed.

Trust in business plumbs the depths

Trust in business has imploded since the banking crisis of 2008, according to Edelman, the public relations company, which has been mapping it for 18 years with its Trust Barometer.[14] In recent years it has reported a crisis of trust around the world in business leaders, as well as politicians, media and non-governmental organizations.

The Barometer has picked up unease among people all over the world who feel the system is biased against them and in favour of the rich and powerful. Credibility of business leaders has slumped, with less than half of those surveyed trusting chief executives to do the right thing. This is a big issue for the business community as it means rising support for anti-business policies such as protectionism, anti-globalization and a retreat from the free market, even if it means slower growth. This supports the view that inequality is driving a wedge between societies worldwide. When influential figures – within business – can afford to opt out of the use of public services and have few points of contact with ordinary people, the social compact starts to break down.

As already mentioned, highly-paid top bosses have the ear of government. They can lobby against a more generous welfare system that would mean higher taxes for those at the top. The fact that many of those helped by welfare payments are in work and could even be part of their own staff, appears to pass them by.

Even some people from within the ranks of the business world are concerned that the current system of executive pay is unsustainable and needs to change. The UK's Investment Association, which represents large investors and shareholders, set up a working group in 2015 to look into remuneration. The working group included the chairman of

Sainsbury's and the group chief executive of Legal & General, one of Britain's largest investing institutions. Nigel Wilson, head of L&G, said the current approach of UK companies to executive pay was 'not fit for purpose'.

Against this backdrop, governments have looked at ways of reining in top pay. But often reform attempts are watered down by opposition from business lobbies and threats to re-locate to more accommodating jurisdictions. The corporate governance movement has had a history of good intentions producing the wrong outcomes and thwarted efforts to change the pay orthodoxy, as we will discuss in the next chapter.

4

Corporate Governance Fights a Losing Battle

Once you start to jail executives for defrauding their companies of expenses for a $6,000 shower curtain and a $17,000 travelling toiletries case, you know there is a serious problem with corporate excess. The public outcry over scandals that saw Dennis Kozlowski sent to jail in 2005 in the US for defrauding nearly $100 million from the company that he ran, and the head of the non-profit New York Stock Exchange, Dick Grasso, chase his $139 million bonus through the courts for five years, forced corporate reforms on to the US agenda. But the road to reform is paved with good intentions and governments have repeatedly made attempts to arrest the soaring incomes of those at the top, or at least pay lip service to some kind of fairness in the distribution of income. Many efforts have backfired and led to even higher rewards.

Corporate Governance Fights a Losing Battle

Attempts to rein in pay

President Bill Clinton tried to stop soaring executive remuneration in 1993 when he effectively set a $1 million limit on directors' pay by making anything above that level non-tax deductible for companies. However, in the small print of his legislation was a clause that specified payments with performance conditions were exempt from the $1 million rule. That effectively meant company boards boosted all salaries to $1 million and paid bonuses and extras in stock options that directors could cash in for shares at a later date. This prompted an explosion in executive awards and, as share prices picked up sharply with the 1990s stock market boom, executives were cashing in enormous packages. In 1991, average US CEO pay was $2.6 million, rising to $9 million a decade later. By 2016 it was $13.1 million.

Similarly, a well-meaning attempt by the European Union to crack down on bank bonuses in the wake of the financial crisis has actually led to an increase in bankers' fixed pay. Brussels ruled in 2013 that big EU banks could pay only 100 per cent of salary to bankers as a bonus – or 200 per cent with prior shareholder approval. That meant banks just increased salaries to get around it.

Attempts at reform of executive pay in the UK

began in the early 1990s. In the most high-profile protest about corporate excess, unions dragged a pig named Cedric and a trough to the British Gas annual shareholders' meeting in 1994 to protest about a 75 per cent pay rise for chief executive Cedric Brown. His package was – by today's standards – a modest £475,000, but the company was newly-privatized and making staff redundant, and it had generated a lot of public anger.

A classic response to public anger in the UK was to commission a corporate governance review of company practices by a member of the great and the good. These followed hot on the heels of each other in the 1990s, starting with Sir Adrian Cadbury in 1992. The problem with these corporate governance reforms was that they tried to establish best practice and were not binding. Also, they shied away from anything radical, not surprisingly given that they were usually run by a corporate heavyweight who did not want to rock the boat. The late Sir Richard Greenbury, former chair of Marks & Spencer, who ran an inquiry into executive pay in 1995, said it was the worst year of his life. He did not like the press scrutiny or being attacked by business for suggesting more red tape and the unions for failing to tackle excess awards.

Legal reform in the US and corporate governance

changes in the UK also put the onus for policing executive pay more and more onto shareholders, who were not always eager to pick up the baton. They also sought to link pay more closely with performance, arguing that if companies were not thriving, neither should their leaders. This backfired spectacularly as shareholders did not step up to man the awards consistently, and the entrenchment of performance pay pushed executive packages even higher, as we have seen in previous chapters. At the turn of the millennium when UK phone company Vodafone took over its German rival, Mannesmann for $181 billion – the largest corporate deal in history – its boss Sir Christopher Gent received a special pay deal of $10 million to reflect the success. However, the merger went badly wrong and is now taught as a case study in business schools as one of the most value-destroying takeovers in the corporate world. Sir Christopher said in 2003 that he should have told the board his US-style pay deal 'was a bridge too far'.[1]

New Companies Act

The drive to reform corporate governance saw Tony Blair's Labour government launch a new

Companies Act in 2006. And the interest in tackling pay, inequality and the corporate world continues to the present day, with Theresa May's ministers producing new recommendations in 2017. But this collection of well-meaning efforts and reports did little to reverse or even slow down the trend towards growth in excessive remuneration.

With the 2006 Companies Act, the longest piece of legislation to be passed into British law (up to that point), Britain's Labour government tried to go beyond shareholder value in its definition of a company's purpose. Section 172 of the Companies Act, which is the basis for public company law in the UK, states quite clearly: 'A director of a company must act in the way he considers, in good faith, would be most likely to promote the success of the company for the benefit of its members as a whole, and in doing so have regard (amongst other matters) to ...'.

The list of items to which the director must have regard, includes: the likely consequences of any decision in the long term; the interests of employees; the need to foster good relationships with suppliers, customers and others; the impact of the company's operations on the community and environment; the desirability of the company maintaining high standards of conduct; and the need to act fairly as between members of the company. Unfortunately, this clause has not been given the prominence it deserves. It is often disregarded by directors, or worse, not even known about. There has never been a concerted effort to enforce it. Ask many non-executive directors about their role and they will repeat the mantra that they are running the company to create value for shareholders. Sir Vince Cable, leader of the UK's Liberal Democrats says: 'I suspect most directors have never looked up their legal obligations. I suspect they'd get a shock as you don't see these things reflected in the corporate world.'

It is worth asking whether there was ever any intention of moving towards a more stakeholder model for the economy, and whether the Companies Act papered over the divisions in the Labour government between those who wanted to clamp down on the corporate sector and those who were happy with the status quo.

In fact, Tony Blair's Labour government that came to power in 1997 with an agenda for social reform was more than happy to leave the responsibility for corporate leadership to the shareholders. New Labour had gone on a charm offensive towards the business community before it was elected and was unwilling to upset its new allies with any reforming zeal.

Are Chief Executives Overpaid?

Lord Mandelson, Labour's business secretary in 1998, summed up the party's embrace of free markets and the City when he famously said he was 'intensely relaxed about people getting filthy rich as long as they pay their taxes'. In this way, New Labour distanced itself from previous Labour administrations which had been suspicious of free markets and the business class. It left shareholders to police any overpaying of the businessmen it was cosying up to.

Like it or not, shareholders have been placed at the heart of corporate governance – the company is run for them and they must monitor it and police the directors' pay awards. They have been given a series of increasing powers in order to do this even though they are often reluctant policemen.

Say on pay

Shareholders are the ones with the power to hold directors to account on pay if they choose to do so. In the UK, they were given a so-called 'say on pay' in 2003 – a non-binding vote on the company's remuneration report each year. In addition, they have a vote on the board directors – whether to renew their tenure.

In the US, shareholders were accorded the power for a similar advisory vote on pay in the Dodd-Frank Act after the financial crisis. This was implemented in 2011; however, *The New York Times* calculated in 2015 that since the votes were tallied, CEO pay had risen by 12 per cent a year.[2] The shareholder votes are not binding, but few companies want to fall out publicly with their investors, and it was envisaged that even an advisory vote would prompt changes. However, since these votes were sometimes ignored by companies, the government decided to go a step further in the UK.

As part of the reforms that were introduced by former UK business secretary Sir Vince Cable in 2013, shareholders now have a binding vote on the company's pay policy every three years. This is a potentially powerful tool if investors choose to exercise it, as it means they can dispute a pay strategy and actively throw it out by a 75 per cent majority vote. Of course, this seldom happens. Shareholders will say it reflects a breakdown in trust and a deterioration in their relationship with the company if they have to resort to voting against a motion. They like to work behind the scenes in conversations with the chairperson, the remuneration committee and the remuneration consultants to agree a pay policy that is suitable. Obviously, this approach is hard to assess as, by necessity, it is behind-the-scenes, but from time to time disputes burst out into the open.

Shareholder Spring

For those who are keen to see shareholders take the leading role in monitoring company pay, they were encouraged by a flowering of investor activism in 2012. Shareholders on both sides of the Atlantic suddenly found a voice after executive pay rose sharply during a turbulent period for the world economy. In Britain, investors voted against remuneration at five top companies and ousted three chief executives – at insurance group Aviva, pharmaceuticals company Astra Zeneca, and newspaper group, Trinity Mirror.

In the US, investors voted against pay at Citigroup after the board proposed paying the chief executive some $15 million in a year when the bank's shares nearly halved. Protestors were escorted out of GE's annual meeting in Detroit in a loud protest about pay and tax policies. The press dubbed the shareholder uprising 'the Shareholder Spring' after the unrest in the Arab world which saw several governments topple. However, like the Arab Spring, the shareholder one fizzled out and, while pay disputes at individual companies continue to make the head-lines, there has been no real concerted effort by shareholders to institute a broader set of changes.

It is unrealistic to think we can rely on sharehold-ers to effect lasting change to the executive pay climate. Many believe it is unfair of governments to place them in the front line of social and economic policy in this way. After all, however large a chief executive's package, it can be a small fraction of the profits at a big multinational company, and inves-tors have other issues to focus on.

Shareholders are not the only ones

Many share the view that the focus on shareholders has gone too far. In a recent report, think-tank IPPR is highly critical of shareholder-based governance, saying it is 'not well founded in either theory or practice'.[3]

Shareholders' role in governance is open to a number of criticisms. Companies are not legally 'owned' by shareholders (in strict legal terms, they own the shares, not the company) and there is no reason why investors should have control rights over companies. The changing nature of share own-ership also means that many investors are holding shares for very short periods and have little interest in stewardship of the company.

Share ownership is very different today from the era when shares were owned by individuals or even national institutions and pension funds who bought into the company and held onto the shares for several years. Many big fund managers are now global and the average length of time a share is held is under six months. Many shares are traded swiftly by computers – within milliseconds – and controlled by algorithms. These changes have given rise to the 'ownerless corporation', where few or no shareholders have significant holdings and few, therefore, have either the power or incentive to exercise effective control.

The relationship between shareholders and directors is too cosy and informal – there is little chance for outsiders to find out what goes on in the behind-the-scenes meetings. There is also a feeling that big investment funds that now hold most shares have a conflict of interest in pay discussions as their own fund managers and executives are extremely well paid themselves.

Big investment funds and shareholder groups used to invest a lot of money and attention in their governance departments where experts would interact with companies, giving them feedback and engaging with directors. However, many have faced cutbacks in this area as it makes no profit, and now engagement is often delegated to the fund managers themselves who are essentially considering whether to buy or sell. If shareholders do not like what a company is doing, they are increasingly likely to vote with their feet and sell the shares rather than engage for change.

Shareholder primacy also fails to recognize the role played by employees in a firm. Shareholders do not bear the most risk – they can diversify their holdings – whereas employees' risk is much greater in that they generally only have one job. But in terms of formal participation and governance rights for employees, the UK comes sixth from bottom among EU countries.

German lessons

In Germany, the workforce is very much part of the debate about executive pay and, indeed, business decisions in general, because of the way companies are organized. This means that the German model of corporate governance is often held up as a solution to the issue of excessive pay in the UK and US. There are clear advantages to the German system, but it should not be seen as a panacea, not least because executive pay is creeping up there too.

The German corporate system mandates two-tier boards for all big companies. That means there is a supervisory board that oversees the management board. That board consists of an equal number of shareholder representatives and elected employee members. The chairman is a shareholder and has a casting vote on all decisions, but generally the board strives to reach a consensus.

The supervisory board is a route for employees to air grievances, but also to contribute to important decisions. When we interviewed employee representatives in 2013,[4] Martina Klee from Deutsche Bank's supervisory board told us: 'My expertise is to tell the board what issues really touch the workforce and what they think.'

After the financial crisis, the supervisory board was given the additional power of setting executive pay. In 2012, in one of the first instances of a supervisory board exercising its new might, the staff representatives led a move to reduce the package for Martin Winterkorn, the then chief executive of Volkswagen by 20 per cent, even though it was a year in which the carmaker had done extremely well. The employees felt it was insensitive to be paying him so much at a time of national austerity and managed to convince the shareholders to vote with them. VW has not turned out to be a model of good corporate governance, however, and for the past couple of years, it has been engulfed in an emissions scandal that has led to high-profile resignations and could still result in criminal prosecutions. And pay for chief executives in Germany is now on average around €5 million – some way behind the US, but generally in line with the UK.

In the German election campaign of 2017, the left-of-centre SPD party put forward proposals for reforming executive pay by restricting the tax deductibility of directors' pay to €500,000 and giving shareholders the right to set a maximum ratio for top pay to average salaries at a company. These proposals were popular with the public, but not enough to get the SPD elected on its own, although it later joined a coalition government.

Another development overseas that is worth consideration is the Australian two-strikes rule. This has been in place since 2012 and means that if more than a quarter of shareholders cast a vote against the company's remuneration report two years in a row, the entire board of directors has to face a re-election vote. It makes it hard for boards to ignore investor protests about pay and has led to better engagement.

Are Chief Executives Overpaid?

Another attempt at change: 2013 reforms

After the so-called Shareholder Spring in 2012, there was momentum for a change in the law to the pay rules in Britain. There was also a growing interest in the German model and a desire to give employees more of a voice on top pay. Sir Vince Cable, business secretary in the new coalition government, said he was committed to an end of 'payment for failure'.

As part of the reforms, the government considered introducing the inclusion of employees on remuneration committees or on boards so that they could be consulted on bosses' remuneration. However, this proved universally unpopular with business leaders and the bill only required companies to show how they had compared executive pay rises to those of the workforce.

After starting out with fairly ambitious goals, the Business, Enterprise and Regulatory Reform Act (2013) had been watered down considerably by opposition from the corporate sector. In the end, it relied on the time-honoured tradition of bolstering the powers of shareholders. By November 2017, Sir Vince said he was sympathetic to the view that 'we should have gone further in 2013 and should still go further'. He felt that he should have pressed on with the proposal for workers on boards, in particular.

Nevertheless, the new rules have had an effect. The requirement that companies produce a single figure for chief executive pay in a particular year, with guidelines on how to calculate that, have increased transparency. One of the most significant changes was to give shareholders a binding vote every three years on pay policy in addition to their existing annual advisory vote on the remuneration report. All payments, including exit payments, are covered by the new vote.

Although at first it seemed as though this binding vote would be a damp squib, it has proved important in some cases and it has focused the attention of companies who might be tempted to manipulate their performance goals. In conjunction with this binding vote, companies are also required to make their performance metrics clearer and more understandable. They also have to present a table about how much will be paid out for certain levels of performance, which is meant to make the remuneration report easier to understand and in an accessible format.

These reforms were aimed at simplifying the multiple pages of the remuneration report contained in a company's annual report, but they have done little to address the complexity of executive pay. Shareholders still criticize top pay for its many different elements and its complex nature.

Investors look at reform

With this in mind, the Investment Association – Britain's representative body for shareholders with £5.5 trillion under investment – set up an Executive Remuneration Working Group in September 2015. The organization said it wanted to bring forward proposals for a radical simplification in executive pay at UK-listed companies.

'Complex pay structures can make it difficult for investors and the wider community to judge whether high rewards are being earned for exceptional management performance or mediocre performance flattered by favourable external factors', the group said at the time. However, by the time the group issued its final report in July 2016, the drive towards dramatic simplification had largely been lost as Investment Association members wanted more flexibility around remuneration. The group issued ten recommendations with the first recommendation stating that remuneration committees should have more flexibility to set remuneration structures that are most appropriate to the company's strategy and needs.

It calls for more transparency, the requirement for whole boards, and particularly chairpersons, to be involved in the remuneration process and a call for boards to explain why they have set a particular pay level with regard to pay ratios. However, once flexibility is introduced in setting pay, the move is often towards more complexity rather than less.

As we have seen in this chapter, shareholders have largely been ineffective in addressing rising executive remuneration and the huge pay gaps that divide society. Even governments with reform at their heart have failed to institute meaningful, lasting changes. Companies have managed to evade many reform attempts, either by gaming the guidelines or ignoring them. The corporate sector still benefits from the sort of self-regulation that has been squeezed out from other parts of the economy. Companies have successfully resisted more draconian interventions either through unbiased regulation or company law.

Shareholders should not be the ones to hold companies to account. Companies are the construct of society with an important role to play that goes much further than being used as cash machines to produce dividends for investors. This means that chief executives need to be required to operate in a different way, and that should be reflected in the way they are paid. In the next chapter, I will look at how this can be changed.

5

What Can Be Done?

In order to address the continuing injustice of executive excess, we need to introduce lasting structural changes that can tackle the deep underlying causes and imbalances of power contributing to these huge pay awards.

There have been suggestions of a maximum pay cap and a legislative crackdown on top pay, but since so many reform attempts have been the victims of unforeseen consequences in the past, we should hesitate before adopting rules that can be gamed by the companies involved.

Business leaders need to rise to the challenge – many will admit privately that the system is unsustainable and needs to change, but will not stand up in public and say it. With distrust of the corporate sector at an all-time high, their inertia could backfire on them and the companies they run.

Are Chief Executives Overpaid?

There is a very real threat of a backlash against wide pay disparities, and we are already seeing the growth in support for anti-business policies such as protectionism.

If some meaningful changes in the way we pay our executives can be achieved, we can start to reverse the inexorable upwards trend in remuneration at the top and the anger it fosters. At the same time, we can encourage companies to work in a more inclusive way to the benefit of all of us.

Top tax rates should rise

One of the obvious ways to address excessive pay is to raise taxes on top incomes and wealth. This is anathema to most Western governments, which have slashed tax rates for the rich and argued strongly that to raise them would be harmful to the economy. But it is worth remembering that tax rates in the UK and US are at historically low levels. Even the free-market International Monetary Fund which has long pushed a low-tax argument, has done an about-turn. The fund said in 2017 that cutting tax for the top 1 per cent had gone too far and that rich countries could raise top rates of tax without damaging growth.

What Can Be Done?

Taxes have become markedly less progressive since the 1980s, with the average top rate in the rich countries of the OECD falling from 62 per cent in 1981 to 35 per cent thirty years later. At the same time, income is taxed at twice the rate of capital gains, which is a more significant levy for many with large investments. This means the rich have thrived in the decade since the financial crisis. In the US, the top 1 per cent have seen their income grow twenty-five times more than the rest of the population since 2008 – taking some 85 per cent of the increase in income during that decade.

In the UK, those households with income of £275,000 or more had quickly recovered from the slump brought on by the banking crisis, and their share of national income had returned to the level of pre-2007, according to research by the Resolution Foundation. But the other 99 per cent of UK households have not fared so well, with low- to middle-income households seeing their income fall.

Another part of the debate on taxes is the need to close loopholes that enable the wealthy and big corporations to shelter their income in offshore jurisdictions. Writing in *The Guardian*, Aditya Chakrabortty points to the link between wealthy individuals who shelter from tax offshore, and the political system that sets the policies for everyone.

'Our democracy is a bidders' market in which the super-rich can determine the lives of us, the little people.' 'We must accept that Big Finance and runaway inequality are incompatible with either a functioning democracy or a sustainable economy.'[1]

Nevertheless, successive UK and US governments have shied away from raising tax rates. David Cameron, Conservative prime minister of the UK coalition government in 2010, was quick to scrap the 50p top rate of tax that was briefly imposed in April 2010 by Gordon Brown's Labour administration to help pay for the banking crisis.

Donald Trump has passed an extensive tax bill in the US that marks the biggest changes to the tax base since Ronald Reagan's reforms in 1986, slashing top rates in a direct benefit to the wealthy. The bill includes a deep cut to corporate taxes from 35 per cent to 21 per cent. Unions and campaigners have strongly argued for some of those tax breaks to be passed on to the workforce and a handful of companies have increased wages, but this has not been widespread.

While higher rates of tax for top earners, such as that suggested by Labour leader Jeremy Corbyn in the 2017 election campaign, are often lambasted by political rivals, they can be popular with the public. It is not radical to ask those with the deepest pockets to contribute more, especially as they have benefitted so much from the current economic set-up.

Higher top rates of tax have got to be part of the overall solution to inequality but will not solve things on their own. There is currently discussion in the US around cracking down on corporate tax evasion and introducing a luxury tax for top earners, but these are unlikely to be advocated by President Trump.

Furthermore, we need to change the rhetoric around tax – contributions should be seen as a badge of honour and the sign of a healthy society, rather than a cost to be avoided. After all, the corporate sector benefits from the societal improvements that are achieved with higher tax rates such as infrastructure spending, better education and healthcare, so should not shirk their responsibilities in paying them.

A tax rise can often be avoided by those wealthy enough to employ top accountants, but this needs to be publicly condemned. One way of shining more light on the tax debate would be to publish tax returns online – a practice that is the norm in Sweden.

Are Chief Executives Overpaid?

Caring capitalism

Raising taxes may be one way to encourage companies to stop paying top dollar, but if we could shift the focus of the corporate sector beyond purely achieving returns for shareholders, we could start to address more of the imbalances within the workplace.

Professor Colin Mayer has argued in his book *Firm Commitment* that the modern corporation is failing the public and needs to be replaced by structures that build more trust. The current economic model of the corporation ignores the broader part it can play in society. He says that 'Owners and directors should not stick rigidly to particular arrangements. They should recognize the need for flexibility and adaptation of values, ownership and boards over time.' This may not sound as if it is about pay, but it is important to re-think the corporate world if we are to address pay inequalities. A sticking plaster of another corporate governance review or an additional piece of data is not going to change behaviour significantly. But if executives and shareholders are given different objectives and companies are constructed in new ways, we could achieve a radical transformation of the business world.

Whether we call this a stakeholder approach or caring capitalism, it is nothing short of a new corporate ethos. We are starting to see some tentative steps emerging. For example, the Benefit Corporation movement that started in the US gives for-profit corporate entities new legal goals. These include a positive impact on society, workers, community and the environment, rather than just profit maximization for shareholders.

Other smaller companies – often technology firms – are introducing low pay ratios or getting their employees to vote on the right level of pay for the boss. A Canadian initiative, Wagemark, was set up in 2014 to give an endorsement to companies with fair pay ratios. It aims to set a kitemark for best practice in pay. Similarly, the Living Wage Foundation in Britain endorses employers that pay the living, rather than minimum wage.

These are very encouraging moves, but so far they represent tiny initiatives and generally do not apply to large organizations. We have to take a new look at the corporate structures that have existed since the end of the Second World War and make moves to overhaul them. This is a big ask, but we could start by setting new goals for executives. In the UK, the purpose of the corporation is already enshrined in the 2006 Companies Act and directors need reminding of that. We already have the legislation in place, but it needs to be enforced.

Are Chief Executives Overpaid?

New watchdog

A stakeholder focus is being considered by the Financial Reporting Council, the UK's corporate governance watchdog, in its consultations on a new governance code that could entrench the Companies Act provisions. This is an important first step, as is the recognition by the watchdog that it cannot currently investigate and prosecute company directors who are not accountants or actuaries – a lack that should be addressed. The consultation on a new code will be completed in 2018, but the depth of the problem around excessive pay actually calls for a more robust intervention. The Financial Reporting Council is dominated by an accountancy outlook on the world and that skews decision-making.

In the US – beyond the legalities – corporate governance has been left to shareholders to enforce. But with such a large and diverse body of investors, there is not even any agreement on what the guidelines should be. In fact, in 2017 two groups of shareholders signed up to differing codes on the principles of governance. Without a broad enough coalition among shareholders as to what constitutes good governance, it is little wonder that boards find it easy to ignore their protestations.

Both countries would benefit from a new statutory body, focused purely on company governance, the role of directors and corporate accountability. The new organizations would be distinct from the market listing authorities such as the Securities and Exchange Commission (SEC) in the US and the London Stock Exchange since these do not enforce governance. The onus would then be on the new institutions to establish some clear guidelines that could be enforced and entrenched without relying on the whim of shareholders.

A new emphasis on corporate governance would start to shift the business community towards a more inclusive focus. If we are to achieve a new sort of capitalism, we need to turn our companies from short-term profit-making machines for shareholders into long-term investors in the skills and wages of the workforce, the sustainability of the environment, as well as longer-term returns for investors.

Pushing for pay reform

There is no shortage of calls for pay reform and corporate governance changes, but most proposals involve tweaking the existing system rather than overhauling it.

In the UK, MPs called for a more inclusive

approach in their report on corporate governance in March 2017, where they stressed that they were trying to ensure the better enforcement of the 2006 Companies Act: 'to improve the voice of other stakeholders, including employees, and to require companies to engage in a more open and transparent manner with the public.' The MPs did recommend some fairly bold solutions such as the phasing out of LTIPs. No new LTIPs should be agreed from the start of 2018 and existing arrangements should not be renewed, they recommended. The MPs want the Financial Reporting Council to work with stakeholders to establish deferred stock rather than LTIPs as a way of encouraging long-term decision-making.

The US is a step further away from this level of reform since many remuneration plans are still focused on stock options. Recent calls for change are directed towards the award of shares rather than options in order to institute a longer-term focus. Some shareholders also favour strong clawback provisions, but not everyone agrees.

In order to improve engagement with shareholders, the British MPs said the corporate governance code should be revised to give investors a binding vote on executive pay awards the year after 25 per cent of investors vote against the remuneration report. Binding votes are often discussed on both sides of the Atlantic, but some shareholders warn they will be less likely to vote if it is binding. As already mentioned, they are wary of becoming proxy company directors.

Theresa May's turn

Theresa May, Britain's prime minister, often talks about creating a country that works for everyone. In her campaign speech before becoming prime minister, she had criticized 'an irrational, unhealthy and growing gap between what the companies pay their workers and what they pay their bosses.' She had even mentioned putting workers on boards: 'If I'm prime minister . . . we're going to have not just consumers represented on company boards, but workers as well.' Similarly, before his election, Donald Trump called high executive pay a 'complete joke', but said he couldn't do anything about it because of the free enterprise system. As with so many good intentions among politicians, Mrs May has also since rowed back from her initial enthusiasm about reform of company boards and restricted her proposals to the publication of pay ratios and other transparency steps.

Are Chief Executives Overpaid?

After she was weakened by her failure to gain a decisive majority in the election of 2017, her business secretary, Greg Clark, published a paper of reforms to address excessive executive pay levels. The promised inclusion of workers on boards was missing, however. Also watered down was a proposal for a binding vote each year on pay. The government is now introducing an annual register to name and shame companies where pay votes fall below 80 per cent support.

The publication of the pay ratio between executive pay and average workforce wages – to be introduced in 2018 – is a useful step forward in highlighting the large pay gaps that exist. The policy was advocated strongly by the High Pay Centre, which believes that transparency around the ratio may concentrate the minds of investors, the workforce and the public, and could lead to some intervention towards reducing that gap.

But there is some scepticism about whether the current reforms will have the benefits that Mrs May envisages. Instead of the requirement to include workers on boards and give them a vote on executive pay awards, the reforms say that companies should consult with the workforce over pay – either by putting workers on boards, nominating a non-executive director to talk to the staff or consulting an employee advisory council, but crucially it is left to the individual company to interpret this in its own way.

These reforms only go so far and are likely to have minimal effect. Unfortunately, Mrs May's government has become consumed by the Brexit debate with little time, energy and will for radical reforms in the corporate sector.

Workers on remuneration committees

Many of those in favour of greater workplace democracy in the corporate world argue for the adoption of the German two-tier board system, or at least for the inclusion of employees on boards. The UK and US stand out for their lack of employee involvement in boardroom decisions. This has long been an important focus for the High Pay Centre.

Most European countries mandate some form of workers' representation, either on the main board (in a unitary board system) or via a supervisory board. Among Anglo-Saxon companies, however, employee representation at the top table is minimal. The UK has one Anglo-American FTSE 100 company that has an employee board member – First Group, the trains and buses firm – but it comes close to the bottom of the European league table for workforce representation. There are a few companies in the US that have boardroom seats for workers – largely where big employee stock ownership plans have mandated a board place.

As part of the proposed structural changes to executive pay outlined here, employees should be elected to the remuneration committee and to the board. The reasoning is that employees on the remuneration committee would inject some common sense thinking into deliberations on executive pay and remind the board members that the workforce had not had a pay rise, or certainly would not get a rise anything like that under consideration for the chief executive.

Workers on remuneration committees could also organize a company-wide vote on executive pay. Since shareholders have an advisory vote, why not give the workforce equal powers? A more dramatic measure would be to make the workforce vote binding. This would be anathema to executives, but it could make them justify why they are worth millions to the people they are working alongside and would be a useful move to improve corporate democracy. The inclusion of worker representatives in any sort of boardroom setting is seen as radical to the business community, which has strongly resisted any such move. It would also be hard to graft employee democracy on at the top of an organization without the supporting infrastructure. In Germany, a network of workers' councils at all levels feeds into the top echelon of supervisory board members and critics argue that, without a similar tradition in the UK and US, worker board members would be tokenistic and ineffective.

This means we need to overhaul corporate democracy, with the voice of the workforce injected into all levels of decision-making in Anglo-Saxon companies. This can be done by establishing advisory councils and other representative bodies throughout an organization. These would feed into decision-making about pay and other issues – channelling the voice of the employees up to their representatives on the board. This would be a clear improvement in the way companies are currently constructed in the US and UK. All companies claim their workforce as a great asset, but few want to listen to what they have to say. We would find our companies run much more effectively if such a move were adopted.

How many times more?

What the workforce might want to say, if it got the chance, is that it is struggling with a squeeze on wages. As wages for the general workforce have stagnated, pay ratios have become a hot political topic on both sides of the Atlantic.

The idea of the ratio – either top to bottom or top to average – as a measure of corporate fairness has a long history. Plato suggested no-one should get more than five times the norm in ancient Greece, and George Orwell, writing in 1941 said: 'There is no reason that ten to one should not be the maximum normal variation. And within those limits some sense of equality is possible.'

In the 1970s, US management expert Peter Drucker maintained that 20 to one from top to average was the right ratio. However, we have moved a long way from that. In the US in 1965, the ratio was – on average – 20 to 1, but from that period, chief executive pay rose by almost 1,000 per cent while workforce wages went up only 11 per cent[2] and the ratio today is 347 to 1. The UK has been on a similar trajectory with the average ratio for the FTSE 100 now at 129 to 1.

In response to the financial crisis, the US passed the Dodd-Frank Act, setting out a series of new rules on financial regulation. Crucially, it mandated that companies should publish a ratio of top pay to average. This was a reform that was much disputed by the business sector, who argued about it for years. The markets regulator, the SEC, said it was the hardest piece of financial regulation it had ever had to authorize. Finally, companies and the SEC agreed a method for calculating pay ratios after seven years of wrangling and it was implemented in 2018. But Donald Trump is committed to repealing the Act, so it is not clear whether the pay ratio rule will survive.

The UK is committed to introducing the publication of the ratio of top to average wages based on the British workforce in 2018.

Sticking to a ratio

There are some businesses that stick to a fixed ratio such as John Lewis, the retail partnership in the UK where the ratio of top pay to average workforce salary is fixed at 75 to 1. While this may sound high, it is well below the norm for big retailers. Writing for the High Pay Centre in 2015, Jane Burgess, partners' counsellor at John Lewis, said: 'Whilst the pay ratio may narrow the pool of candidates at the senior level, it guarantees that those who join the partnership share a stronger motivation than personal reward: they share the values of the business.'[3]

Whole Foods, the much-smaller US ethical super-markets group, also operated a pay cap in that no-one could earn more than 19 times the average worker's pay. John Mackey, founder and chief executive, decided to forego his salary a decade ago as he retained part of his shareholding and said he was wealthy enough. However, since Whole Foods was taken over by Amazon in 2017, it is unlikely the ratio will remain.

Both John Lewis and Whole Foods are not large international businesses so have little requirement to calculate ratios across borders. One of the arguments against exposing the pay ratio is that pay norms in other countries skew the average when calculated across the workforce, making the final figure meaningless.

The current proposal by Theresa May's Conservative government in the UK is for the ratio to be calculated using data from the British work-force, and similarly the SEC has allowed companies to elect to ignore international rates when calculating their ratios. The ratio of top to average should then be published in the company's annual report.

While the publication of a ratio will add an important piece of information to the remuneration report, it is unlikely to reduce top pay. But the publication of official ratios is likely to lead to some interesting comparisons between companies in the same sector. If you are an ethical shopper, for example, would you change your habits and shop at Waitrose (part of the John Lewis group) where the boss gets paid significantly less than Tesco's or Sainsbury's heads, who receive 345 and 191 times the average, respectively? It could well be used by campaigners to highlight best practice and encourage shoppers to vote with their feet. This, of course, only works with customer-focused businesses.

The direction taken by the pay ratio over time could prompt some interesting questions from employees and shareholders. If there is a big jump in the ratio, should that be a cause for concern? It could mean a big increase in the package for the top boss or a drop in the relative wages at the bottom. It could also have an impact on company morale and productivity.

Some people would like to go further than the publication of the existing ratio to a mandated ratio that firms are not allowed to exceed. Switzerland had a nationwide referendum in 2013 on the introduction of a 12 to 1 pay ratio. But when some top companies threatened to move overseas, the idea was defeated. Also, like many corporate governance fixes, a mandated ratio could have perverse consequences. An investment bank, for example, would have a fairly low pay ratio as most of its bankers are well paid and it outsources the rest of its services.

Companies could be encouraged to outsource services such as cleaning and other support operations so that the low pay of their workers is not included in their ratio – making conditions for those low-paid individuals worse. In fact, John Lewis came under fire several years ago for not including its own cleaners in the pay ratio calculation as they were working for an outsourced contractor.

A mandated ratio could also encourage companies to get around the ratio itself by offering other benefits to the boss that might not be so transparent. Ratios in different sectors are also wildly at odds with each other and it would be hard to find a one-size-fits-all figure.

These issues are not insurmountable. Workers who do the bulk of their labour for a particular company could be included in the ratio even though they work for a contractor. And companies would have to establish the monetary value of any perks offered to the chief executive for inclusion in the calculation.

Jane Burgess says setting a ratio is not an exact science. 'It relies on discretion and judgement and there are challenges to transposing a ratio across businesses and sectors. Similarly, there is no definitive view on the "correct" measure and the pay ratio employed by the Partnership benefits from ongoing scrutiny.' It is at least a first step to require companies to publish their ratios.

Procurement power

While critics are quick to dismiss the publication of pay ratios as another meaningless figure, they can be used in interesting ways. They give national, state and local governments market power over companies seeking contracts with them.

Jeremy Corbyn, Labour leader, has suggested that companies bidding for government contracts should be subject to a maximum wage cap – meeting a 20 to 1 pay ratio between top and bottom. At the beginning of 2017, Mr Corbyn said 'A 20:1 ratio means someone earning the living wage, just over £16,000 a year, would permit an executive to be earning nearly £350,000. It cannot be right if companies are getting public money that can be creamed off by a few at the top.'[4] This would mean huge pay cuts for those leading outsourcing companies such as Capita and G4S who run security services and other public functions. The boss of private security firm G4S was paid £4.8 million in 2016, and Andy Parker, who ran Capita until he stepped down in September 2017, received £2.4 million the same year, while the average wage in the UK remains £28,000.

In the light of this, Mr Corbyn's ratio is a stretch for most companies. Business lobby groups reacted swiftly to dismiss the proposal, with the Institute of Directors calling it a 'non-starter'. But if a future Labour government were serious about tackling the issue this way, the ratio could be set higher and gradually reduced. In fact, another outsourcing company, Serco, has said it would cut its chief executive's pay by 20 per cent from £2.2 million in light of concerns around high pay for procurement companies.

The British outsourcing market for public services delivered by private companies is worth more than £80 billion a year, which gives the government a fair amount of power as a buyer of services. Similarly, in the US, the federal and state governments have huge market power to wield. The US government used its purchasing power after the financial crisis when President Obama introduced a pay cap for firms which were contracting for federal services. No company could bill for staff time at a rate higher than the president's pay, which at the time was $400,000.

Mr Corbyn has also suggested that businesses

with more equal pay structures could pay less corporation tax. This echoes proposals coming up in some states in America, and voted on in California a couple of years ago, that would have awarded favourable corporation tax rates to companies with low pay ratios. The proposal did not pass the Californian legislature and is fraught with difficulty in making it work but is a creative way of trying to address the issue.

The idea of governments using their market power to influence corporate pay is a powerful one, since coercion has had no effect and shareholders are, at best, erratic in using the powers accorded to them.

Cash is king

There is a strong argument for resolving the escalation of executive remuneration by stripping the issue right back to basics. This means clearing out years' worth of performance-related pay theories and metrics. It means putting top executives on a par with their workforce and paying them in cash – a salary. This is how everyone else is paid so it would immediately simplify executive pay and make the figures much easier to compare with the staff.

Are Chief Executives Overpaid?

There are a lot of staff in permanent positions who receive some sort of performance element to their wages – whether commission payments for sales people or a good performance bonus for office staff. Apart from a sales force who are often on a high proportion of commission, these bonuses are, for most people, a small part of the overall package.

It is not clear that these performance elements within companies actually motivate and reward people for doing the right thing, but that is a much wider debate. There is a growing body of opinion on both sides of the Atlantic that performance pay for top bosses has led to the wrong outcomes and we should get back to cash for all.

In his book, *The CEO Pay Machine*, published in 2017, Steve Clifford, a former chief executive of Seattle-based King Broadcasting, and member of several US remuneration committees, calls for executive pay to be stripped of its performance elements. 'All pay for performance systems cause more harm than good', he says. 'They generate perverse incentives, undeserved and absurdly high bonuses, and damage the companies that use them.'

Peter Montagnon, associate director of the Institute of Business Ethics and a long-time corporate governance expert, argues strongly for cash salaries. He makes an important point, that remuneration committees do not really know what the executive package is worth at the time it is handed over. This is because it is impossible to predict what will happen to the company's share price in the coming years and therefore how much the executive will gain when handed shares or options in the incentive plan. There are financial models that help calculate and predict the value of shares and options in the future, but they are approximate. Mr Montagnon argues 'if you can't value it, you can't give it'.

When executives are paid in cash, companies can require them to buy shares with their salaries if they want them to have a stake in the company. But these shares should be held for the long term – i.e. ten years, even if the executive leaves the company during that time. This will mean that executives must base their decision-making on long-term principles or their own wealth will be at stake. 'Greater clarity and simplification would remove much of the obscurity around the operation of executive pay, which is the cause of much public distrust', Mr Montagnon says.

Cash bonuses

Some reformers are keen to retain a bonus for executives in the form of an annual cash payment that is clearly linked to a certain measure of performance. However, a much better solution would be a bonus as a percentage of salary for all staff, linked to that year's annual profits. This is, again, the John Lewis approach, where each member of staff (or partner) receives the same percentage of their wages as a bonus when there is a good year – the percentage is set each year by the board. Of course, the executives will receive more money than others on lower pay as their salaries are higher to start with, but this idea links the entire workforce in a common endeavour and really does give the feeling that 'we're all in it together'. It gives everyone an incentive to work for the common good of the company.

How much?

While the argument for paying in cash is compelling, there will be another public debate about how much cash those executives should have. Some remuneration consultants have argued that it is fine to pay top bosses in cash as long as the public accepts that £4–5 million is the rate for the job. In that case, cash payments would do little to bring down executive pay, and would, in fact, entrench it, although they would rule out some of the excesses.

What Can Be Done?

Some remuneration consultants have started to talk about the need to pay executives for 'unambiguously outstanding performance'.[5] This is because everyone agrees that payment for failure is wrong, but they say we need a new public debate about the overpayment for mediocre performance.

But this retains the arguments around performance pay. I would maintain that we strip away performance from the discussion. We then come back to what is the right rate for the job? This is not easy to answer and should be the subject of in-depth discussions with boards, the new supervisory body on governance and the workforce representatives.

At the end of the day, the salaries or pay ratios can be voted on by the workforce and shareholders. Once we recalibrate salaries to a reasonable level, we will not have to debate them every year as they will rise in line with workforce wages. We will also free up boards from having to respond to pay scandals every time a big share package pays out.

A new structure

The new structure proposed here would see performance pay stripped back – either so that it doesn't exist at all, or is included in a profits-related bonus that extends to all staff. Executives would then be paid a salary in cash. The level of that salary is more problematic, but with the involvement of all stakeholders, companies should be able to agree on the appropriate level. The job of chief executive is tough and involves a huge commitment. Most people at a company recognize this and are capable of making sensible decisions about pay if trusted with the responsibility.

Executive jobs could be advertised openly rather than touted round to a small number of existing directors by well-rewarded head hunters. This could help open up the talent pool to more people. At the same time, employees in full board positions could make a strong contribution to the direction of the company. If the company and its investors decide that the executive should have a shareholding, then they should buy those shares with their own money and hold them for a long period – beyond their exit from the job.

With the dramatic simplification of pay packages, there should be less need for the industry that exists around corporate pay. The remuneration committee itself would be transformed and become the forum for wide discussions about pay throughout the company, rather than just at the top.

With dramatic changes to the way executives are

paid and a new focus for the company on a wider constituency than just the shareholders, we could create genuine change to the way our form of capitalism works. This would bring benefits for all of us.

Conclusion

The edifice of management pay remains in place with barely a crack. When addressing audiences of businesspeople and executives, I understand why. To question the set-up is to be dangerously radical, an enemy of free markets and even a threat to capitalism itself. However, it is anger over pay, inequality and the current economic set-up that is currently feeding anti-capitalist sentiment among the wider public.

It is important that people feel there is some sense of fairness in the division of rewards throughout the economy or disillusionment sets in. Even free-marketeers can buy in to the idea of pay reform, as greedy executives can be said to be wrecking capitalism for the rest of us. Capitalism as a system has been remarkably successful in improving the lot of a huge number of people, but if a small group of those at the top undermine it by taking more than their fair share, we could face a backlash against free markets.

Stagnating average wages and increasingly insecure employment terms, accompanied by runaway pay at the top, had a role to play in the Brexit vote and the election of Donald Trump in the US. Many people express concerns about the growth of a two-tier economy and society, with the elite enriching themselves at the expense of everyone else.

Commentators such as Martin Wolf in the *Financial Times* argue that the liberal international order that has presided since the Cold War, is crumbling.[1] This is in part because it does not satisfy large parts of western society – the people who voted for Mr Trump and Brexit. As people watch a tiny elite consuming far too much of everything, it undermines their trust in government, business and the country itself. British people therefore ignored warnings about the risks of Brexit and voted Leave in 2016.

In one memorable exchange before the Brexit vote, a journalist quoted a woman in the north-east heckling a visiting professor who encouraged his audience to imagine the plunge in GDP if Britain left the EU. 'That's your bloody GDP, not ours', the woman said.[2] The woman was right in that the enrichment of those at the top has failed to spread beyond that small group in the way that was envisaged in the 1980s.

The trickle-down theory of economics assumed that boosting rewards for people at the top of the income chain would stimulate economic growth as they employed more people and spent their increased income on goods and services. However, the theory has been thoroughly debunked in recent years and disowned by the very institutions that promoted it in the first place, who now say that it has created greater inequality.

A rise in the income share of the wealthiest people actually leads to a fall in growth and, by contrast, a boost to incomes at the bottom increases GDP over the medium term. However, in the past thirty years, the opposite has happened, exacerbating inequality within countries and threatening to unravel the social contract. The absence of trickle down, the growing feeling that business leaders are in it for themselves and the damage to the economy from short-term management incentives, would all indicate that change is required in the way we pay our top bosses.

The deep influence of the business sector has imposed globalization and trade liberalization on a populace that finds it hard to discern the benefits. At the same time, they see the corporate elite hand in glove with governments around the world to ensure there is little challenge to the current set-up.

This reinforces the impression among the public that the system is rigged and the powerful are not just greedy but corrupt as well. These feelings endanger the corporate sector's license to operate, as public faith in business and even capitalism itself is eroded, and support begins to grow for all sorts of anti-business initiatives. Donald Trump has already moved to impose protectionist tariffs on steel imports, threatening to plunge the world into a new, damaging trade war.

A critique of the self-serving justifications for excessive pay is often attacked for relying on the wrong data, a misunderstanding of the way companies work, and plain old envy. But if capitalism is not seen to be fair by much of the public, there will be moves for something more drastic to replace it.

It is time for the business sector to listen to the moderate voices for reform or reap the consequences of growing inequality, anti-business sentiment and possibly more dramatic clashes. If we don't rise to the challenge, the fundamental trust that makes a liberal market democracy function could be damaged beyond repair. We run the risk of sleepwalking into a dystopian future of extreme income disparities and the unrest that could bring.

Notes

Chapter 1 Who Wants To Be a Millionaire?

1 Melanie Kramers, 'More than 80 per cent of new global wealth goes to top 1 per cent while poorest half get nothing'. Oxfam, press release, 22 January 2018. Available at https://www.oxfam.org.uk/med ia-centre/press-releases/2018/01/more-than-80-per-cent-of-new-global-wealth-goes-to-top-1-per-cent-wh ile-poorest-half-get-nothing

2 High Pay Centre, 'It's Fat Cat Day – Thursday Jan 4 2018'. Blog, 4 January 2018. Available at http://highpaycentre.org/blog/its-fat-cat-day-thursday-jan-4-2018

3 CIPD and High Pay Centre, *CIPD/High Pay Centre survey of FTSE100 CEO pay packages*. Available at http://highpaycentre.org/pubs/cipd-high-pay-centre-survey-of-ftse100-ceo-pay-packages-2016

4 AFL-CIO, 'Executive paywatch'. Available at https://aflcio.org/paywatch

5 Margaret Thatcher Foundation, 'Speeches, interviews and other statements'. Available at http://www.margaretthatcher.org/document/105617

6 High Pay Centre, 'The revolving door: how big business has colonised UK politics'. Blog, 25 March 2015. Available at http://highpaycentre.org/blog/the-revolving-door-how-business-has-colonised-uk-politics

7 High Pay Centre, 'The myth of global high pay talent market'. 11 February 2013. Available at http://highpaycentre.org/pubs/the-myth-of-global-high-pay-talent-market

8 High Pay Centre, 'The new closed shop: who's deciding on pay?'. 2 April 2012. Available at http://highpaycentre.org/pubs/publication-the-new-closed-shop-whos-deciding-on-pay

Chapter 2 *Just Deserts?*

1 Simon Goodley, 'Sir Martin Sorrell defends £63m pay package ahead of AGM'. *The Guardian*, 18 April 2016. Available at https://www.theguardian.com/business/2016/apr/18/sir-martin-sorrell-pay-package-agm

2 High Pay Centre, 'Reality bites – average FTSE100 CEO pay package down 17% on previous year'. Blog, 3 August 2017. Available at http://highpaycentre.org/blog/reality-bites-average-ftse100-ceo-pay-package-down-17-on-previous-year

3 High Pay Centre, 'New High Pay Centre report: performance-related pay is nothing of the sort'. 28

October 2014. Available at http://highpaycentre.
org/pubs/new-high-pay-centre-report-performance-
related-pay-is-nothing-of-the-sort

4 High Pay Centre, 'Thinking high and low: exploring pay disparities in society'. 1 September 2015.
Available at http://highpaycentre.org/pubs/thinking-
high-and-low-exploring-pay-disparities-in-society

5 High Pay Centre, 'Made to measure: how opinion
about executive performance becomes fact'. Blog, 15
March 2015. Available at http://highpaycentre.org/
blog/made-to-measure-how-opinion-about-executi
ve-performance-becomes-fact

6 Ibid.

7 Ibid.

8 Ibid.

9 Ibid.

10 2006 Annual Report of Berkshire Hathaway, Inc.

Chapter 3 Why Top Pay Matters

1 Larry Elliott, 'How Much Is Enough? by Robert and
Edward Skidelsky – review'. The Guardian, 29 June
2012. Available at https://www.theguardian.com/
books/2012/jun/29/how-much-is-enough-skidelsky-
review

2 High Pay Centre, 'New High Pay Centre report:
performance-related pay is nothing of the sort'. 28
October 2014. Available at http://highpaycentre.org/
pubs/new-high-pay-centre-report-performance-relat
ed-pay-is-nothing-of-the-sort

3 High Pay Centre, 'Thinking high and low: explor-

ing pay disparities in society'. 1 September 2015. Available at http://highpaycentre.org/pubs/thinking-high-and-low-exploring-pay-disparities-in-society

4 Department for Business Innovation and Skills, 'Kay review of UK equity markets and long-term decision making'. Available at https://www.gov.uk/government/consultations/the-kay-review-of-uk-eq uity-markets-and-long-term-decision-making

5 BBC, 'Barclays' Salz Review blames bank culture', 3 April 2013. Available at http://www.bbc.co.uk/news/business-22012261

6 Financial Times, 'Bonuses Don't Make Bankers Work Harder, says Deutsche's John Cryan'. Available at https://www.ft.com/content/13e676f0-92bb-11e5-94e6-c5413829caa5

7 High Pay Centre, 'Excessive executive pay a threat to business, say Institute of Directors members'. 1 March 2015. Available at http://highpaycentre.org/pubs/excessive-executive-pay-a-threat-to-busine ss-say-institute-of-directors-mem

8 Dan Cable and Freek Vermeulen, 'Stop paying executives for performance'. *Harvard Business Review*, 23 February 2016. Available at https://hbr.org/2016/02/stop-paying-executives-for-performance

9 High Pay Centre, 'If you can't value it, don't pay it', blog. Available at http://highpaycentre.org/blog/if-you-cant-value-it-dont-pay-it

10 TUC, 'UK near the bottom of the global rankings for real wage growth – new TUC analysis finds'. 27 February 2017. Available at https://www.tuc.org.uk/news/uk-near-bottom-global-rankings-

real-wage-growth-%E2%80%93-new-tuc-analysis-finds

11 Hilary Osborne, 'UK workers' wages fell 1% a year between 2008 and 2015, TUC says'. *The Guardian*, 27 February 2017. Available at https://www.theguardian.com/money/2017/feb/27/uk-workers-wages-fall-one-per-cent-year-since-financial-crisis-tuc-analysis

12 CIPD, 'What employees think of their CEO's pay packet'. 1 December 2015. Available at https://www.cipd.co.uk/knowledge/strategy/reward/ceo-pay-report

13 See note 7.

14 https://www.edelman.com/trust-barometer

Chapter 4 Corporate Governance Fights a Losing Battle

1 Dominic White, 'Sir Christopher's biggest regret'. *The Telegraph*, 20 February 2003. Available at http://www.telegraph.co.uk/finance/2843598/Sir-Christophers-biggest-regret.html

2 Gretchen Morgenson, 'Shareholders' votes have done little to curb lavish executive pay'. *The New York Times*, 17 May 2015. Available at https://www.nytimes.com/2015/05/17/business/shareholders-votes-have-done-little-to-curb-lavish-executive-pay.html

3 Mathew Lawrence, *Corporate Governance Reform: Turning Business towards Long-term Success* (London: IPPR, 2017). Available at https://www.ippr.org/publications/corporategovernancereform

4 High Pay Centre, 'Workers on boards: interviews with German employee directors'. 16 September 2013. Available at http://highpaycentre.org/pubs/wor kers-on-boards-interviews-with-German-employee-directors

Chapter 5 What Can Be Done?

1 Aditya Chakrabortty, 'End these offshore games or our democracy will die'. *The Guardian*, 7 November 2017. Available at https://www.theguardian.com/ commentisfree/2017/nov/07/end-offshore-games-democracy-die-paradise-papers

2 Lawrence Mishel and Alyssa Davis, 'Top CEOs make 300 times more than typical workers'. Economic Policy Institute, 21 June 2015. Available at http://www. epi.org/publication/top-ceos-make-300-times-more-than-workers-pay-growth-surpasses-market-gains-and-the-rest-of-the-0-1-percent/

3 High Pay Centre, 'Thinking high and low: exploring pay disparities in society'. 1 September 2015. Available at http://highpaycentre.org/pubs/thinking-high-and-low-exploring-pay-disparities-in-society

4 Rowena Mason, 'Corbyn calls for wage cap on bosses at government contractors'. *The Guardian*, 10 January 2017. Available at https://www.the guardian.com/politics/2017/jan/10/corbyn-proposes-maximum-wage-for-all-government-contractors

5 Julia Kollewe, 'Businesses must alter "toxic" attitude to executive pay, PwC says'. *The Guardian*, 14 July 2016. Available at https://www.theguardian.com/

business/2016/jul/14/businesses-must-alter-toxic-atti
tude-to-executive-pay-pwc-says

Conclusion

1 Martin Wolf, 'The Liberal International Order is Sick'. *Financial Times*, 23 January 2018. Available at https://www.ft.com/content/c45acec8-fd35-11e7-9b 32-d7d59aace167
2 Aditya Chakrabortty, 'One blunt heckler has revealed just how much the UK economy is failing us'. *The Guardian*, 10 January 2017. Available at https://www.theguardian.com/commentisfree/2017/ jan/10/blunt-heckler-economists-failing-us-booming-britain-gdp-london